OBSERVATIONS

ON

THE DISTURBANCES

IN

THE MADRAS ARMY

IN 1809

OBSERVATIONS
ON
THE DISTURBANCES
IN
THE MADRAS ARMY
IN 1809.

IN TWO PARTS.

BY JOHN MALCOLM

GYAN

Published by

Gyan Publishing House
5, Ansari Road
Daryaganj, New Delhi-110002
Phone: 011-47034999, 9811692060
E-mail: books@gyanbooks.com

Distribution Network
gyanbooks.com
India, USA, Canada, UK, Australia, France

ISBN: 978-81-212-8032-7 (PB)
First Published, 1812

2nd Impression 2023

Printed at: Gyan Press, Delhi.

OBSERVATIONS ON THE DISTURBANCES IN THE MADRAS ARMY IN 1809

Author: JOHN MALCOLM

OBSERVATIONS

ON

THE DISTURBANCES

IN

THE MADRAS ARMY

IN 1809

IN TWO PARTS.

BY JOHN MALCOLM,

LIEUTENANT COLONEL IN THE HONOURABLE EAST INDIA COMPANY'S MADRAS ARMY, RESIDENT AT MYSORE, AND LATE ENVOY TO THE COURT OF PERSIA.

LONDON

PRINTED FOR WILLIAM MILLER, ALBEMARLE STREET; AND JOHN MURRAY, FLEET STREET.

1812.

PREFACE

I HAVE hitherto abstained from controversy regarding the late unhappy proceedings at Madras. The part which I had taken in these proceedings had placed me in possession of much information, and I had given a shape to my sentiments upon the subject; but the knowledge of these was limited to a few intimate friends, and to them only under the strictest injunctions of secrecy. I have been applied to more than once for papers and information upon this subject, but have invariably refused; as I deemed it improper to give publicity in any mode to communications, whether verbal or in writing, which had been, at the moment at which they were made, considered as private, or confidential. Nothing could have led me to a departure from this principle but a perusal of the dispatch under date the 10th of September, 1809, from the Government of Fort St. George to the Secret Committee of the Court of Directors, printed by order of the House of Commons. That dispatch contains an implied censure upon my conduct, which nothing but a conviction of its justice could induce me to pass over in silence.

Injustice is aggravated by the power of the individual or body by whom it is committed, and by the want of ability or opportunity in the person who suffers to repel the attack. Had not this dispatch been printed by order of the House of Commons, my character would have secretly received a deep and incurable wound for as it is not likely the Honourable the Court of Directors could have ever thought it possible that so deliberate and grave an authority as the Government of Fort St. George, could (without adequate grounds) have pronounced censure on the character of an officer who stood at the moment as high in rank and trust as the local Government of India had power to raise him*, it becomes probable, that most of those who read this dispatch would be satisfied, without a minute examination of the documents by which it was accompanied: and if any readers went into this detail, and were struck with the remarkable difference between the apparent premises and the conclusions drawn from them, it is more likely they would conclude, that grounds, not yet brought before them, existed, which would warrant the assertions made by Government, than that they should ever suppose the latter had committed such an injustice towards any individual in their service.

I cannot, on this occasion, limit myself to an account of my mission to Masulipatam, which is that part of my conduct to which the Government of Fort St George exclusively refers: justice to my own character demands that I should give a narrative (accompanied by an Appendix of original documents), which will show, in a clear

I was, at the moment this letter was written, at Madras, preparing to proceed on a mission to Persia: not a word even of dissatisfaction at my conduct was expressed—no explanation of any of my acts required; and, consequently, no opportunity afforded of defending myself against the serious charges that were thus secretly transmitted to England. The letter to the Secret Committee is dated the 10th September, 1809, the day before that on which Lord Minto arrived at Madras.

and concise manner, the part I took, and the advice I gave, throughout the whole of those unhappy and guilty proceedings which have lately afflicted our country in India. To render this narrative intelligible to all, I shall prefix a general view of the principal acts of the Government of Fort St. George, from the commencement to the termination of the late violent agitations on the coast. My object in this publication is to vindicate myself, not to attack others. A plain statement of indisputable facts will show, that though my judgment might on some occasions have been wrong, I was invariably actuated by an indefatigable zeal, and an undeviating principle of public duty; that I predicted at the commencement, and at different stages of the proceeding, every event of importance that occurred; that if any one of the many slighted suggestions which I offered had met with attention, the most serious evils would have been averted; and that my efforts were such as ought to have entitled me to the praise and gratitude of those by whom I now find my conduct misrepresented and my character calumniated.

Sir George Barlow has, I observe, from the volume of papers printed by order of the House of Commons, placed upon record a number of my private and confidential communications. This I did not anticipate; and these letters were written in a less guarded style, and with more warmth, than they would have been, if I had foreseen the public use to be made of them. I do not, however, conceive that I have any right to complain of this act: the letters contain not one sentiment of which I am ashamed: they were all on public subjects: and that alone, when they were addressed to Sir George Barlow or his Secretary, rendered them public. But I must claim to myself an equal privilege in bringing forward such private documents as are necessary to prove what I have stated, and to defend myself from those imputations which have been thrown upon my character from a partial, and, I trust I shall prove, a most unfair statement of my conduct when employed at Masulipatam.

I should feel unworthy of that station which I hope I hold in life, if any motive upon earth had such power over my mind as to make me silent under reflections (which I deemed unjust) upon my conduct and where those have been, from any cause, (however unforeseen,) brought before the public, my reply must of course be submitted to the same tribunal This is a circumstance which I by no means regret. Publications in England on the affairs of India have been rare, except on some extraordinary epochs, when attention has been forcibly drawn to that quarter; and a groundless alarm has been spread of the mischiefs which (many conceive) must arise from such free disclosure, and consequent full discussion, of the acts of the Indian Governments. This practice, in my opinion, will have a direct contrary effect. It must always do great and essential good. The nature of our possessions in India makes it necessary that almost absolute power should be given to those entrusted with governments in that quarter; and there cannot be a better or more efficient check over these rulers than that which must be established by the full publicity given to their acts, and the frequent discussion of all their principles of rule. Such a practice will expose imprudence and weakness, however defended by the adherence of powerful friends in England: and it will be more certain to prevent oppression, or injustice, than the general provisions of law, which may be evaded; or the check of superiors, who may, from conceiving the cause of an individual identified with that of authority itself, feel themselves condemned to support proceedings which they cannot approve. This practice, in short, (restrained, as it always must be, by the laws of our country within moderate bounds,) must have the most salutary effects. Its inconveniences are obvious, but trifling when compared to the great and permanent benefits which it must produce : and I am confident that every effort made to repress such discussion is not merely a sacrifice to personal feeling, and to momentary expedience, of one of the best and most operative principles of the British Constitution ; but a direct approximation to the principles of that oriental tyranny, which it is, or ought to be, our chief boast to have destroyed.

PART I

OBSERVATIONS

ON

THE CAUSES AND PROGRESS

OF THE

DISTURBANCES IN THE MADRAS ARMY

OBSERVATIONS, &c.

Some agitation, though of a trifling nature, had prevailed among the Company's officers on the coast establishment from a period as far back as the publication of the Regulations of the year 1796, which they conceived to entitle them to a complete equalization of allowances with the officers of the Bengal establishment. These feelings had little time for operation in the course of that active and brilliant service in which the Madras army was employed during the administration of Lord Wellesley. The increase of establishment rendered necessary to preserve the great accession of territory acquired by that nobleman, occasioned a promotion, that, for a period, silenced their discontent; but that spirit was revived in the year 1805 and 1806, when, in addition to their former grievance, they conceived that there was an evident and injurious partiality shown towards his Majesty's officers, who were said to be promoted to commands and staff situations to the injury of the officers of the Company's service. Addresses to Government and to the Court of Directors were at this period agitated and in circulation; but none, to my knowledge, were brought forward; owing, perhaps, to the orders from the Honourable the Court of Directors, who, it would appear, had, on private representation, adopted some measures to redress those grievances of which the army at that moment complained. This spirit of discontent might have died of itself; or, at all events, it would have been more easily repressed, had not the flame of discord burst out in a higher quarter. The quarrel which occurred between the Governor, Sir George Barlow, and the Commander-in-Chief, General M[c]Dowall, may, no doubt, (as it led to those measures which Government adopted towards the general staff of the coast army,) be deemed the remote source of all the violent and indefensible acts of the army, and in that view merits a short notice. The mind of General M[c]Dowall was much irritated at his not being appointed to council; and he gave way, in consequence, to a language of complaint and discontent, of which, it must be concluded, he could never have calculated the effect. Every act of Government that affected the wishes or interests of either an individual or a class of officers naturally caused complaints, which the Commander-in-Chief certainly did not discourage. He must have thought that the influence and importance of a seat in council would have enabled him more easily to have satisfied or silenced their murmurs; and he cannot be supposed to have felt much sorrow that Government should have experienced the inconvenience of an exclusion which he considered as so great a personal grievance: and when his mind was further irritated by what he deemed to be slight and neglect, on the part of Sir George Barlow, of his rights in his military character of Commander-in-Chief, these feelings had probably a wider action. In the temper which I have shown the coast army was in at this moment, it is not surprising, when they saw such an example of discontent, and felt unrepressed by that high authority which was immediately over them, that they should have been more bold, and that their violence should have taken a more formidable shape towards Government, against which this spirit was, by the proceeding of the Commander-in-Chief, very unadvisedly and inconsiderately, however unintentionally, directed. But if a want of reflection on one part (few will accuse General M[c]Dowall of more than want of reflection) led to such consequences, can we say there was much more wisdom on the other, which, if it did not provoke, never made one attempt to prevent, the occurrence of those evils with which it was threatened? A cold, even, mechanic course of action, which gave great attention to the ordinary rules of public business dignified with the name of public principles, but none to human nature, was opposed at this period to the proceedings of the Commander-in-Chief and the army; and had the effect, which was to be expected, of accelerating that crisis which it was so important to avoid.

It may be here necessary to explain what was meant by the term public principle. It was constantly used at Madras (with some deviation, I conceive, from its highest and most dignified sense) to denote the rules of public business founded either in precedent or in written law, and certainly well adapted for order and convenience in the common course of affairs. But if such rules were sufficient, no talents would be necessary to govern man kind. A copying clerk, or even the regulation-book which he copies, might rule a state. Success in this endeavour (the object of which is to render the task of Government simple and easy) will be always agreeable to the character of the Government. The more despotic that is, the more easily may we preserve inviolate such rules or principles. For though great commotions will occur in the most despotic states, and force their rulers to an occasional deviation from such principles, these deviations will be unfrequent to what must arise in more free and liberal governments, in which that constant attention which it is necessary to pay to men's tempers, and to those pretensions and rights upon which such an order of things is grounded, must produce a much more frequent departure from the exact letter (and sometimes from the spirit) of those unbending rules. It is this fact which renders the task of government so much more difficult in those states than in any others. Any man (who has obsequious slaves to govern) can, if he has memory to recollect the principles of rule, be a despot, or a despot's deputy; but far different qualities are required where the minds of those under authority are of a freer and bolder stamp: over such a society those alone are fit to rule, who, fully informed of all its component parts, can judge the periods when the temporary departure from an established principle will effect more in the cause of authority than its rigid observance; when lenity is more powerful than severity, and mildness and moderation tend more to restore order and to maintain tranquillity, than all the force of a violent government.

The intelligent reader will perceive, that, in contrasting free and despotic governments, I refer exclusively to rules of administration. Laws are, no doubt, more inflexible in free states than in others. But even respecting laws it may be observed, that the general principle prevails: for the legislative power in free states shows a disposition to repeal or modify laws in reference to the interests, the opinions, sometimes even to the prejudices, of great bodies of the people; while the despot has no maxim, but that all must be subject to the authority of Government. There is, no doubt, a great distinction in every community between civil and military bodies: the laws for the government of the latter are, of course, more arbitrary and unbending; but, even in these bodies there is a *national character* that will compel attention. The same principles cannot be applied to an English as a Russian army: and it is when such bodies are in an agitated and convulsed state, that these characteristic distinctions are most prominent and discernible. It is on such emergencies that a statesman will succeed in averting a danger, which will only be increased by every measure of the mere rote follower of public rules. Cicero* has observed, that "it appears to be the dictate of sound "policy, to act in accommodation to particular conjunc-

Cicero's Letters to his Friends, Vol. I. p. 194. Octavo. London, 1753.

" tures, and not obstinately persevere in one invariable " scheme, when the public circumstances, together with " the sentiments of the best and wisest members of the " community, are evidently changed. In conformity to " this notion, the most judicious reasoners on the art of " government have universally condemned an inflexible " perseverance in one uniform tenor of measures. The " skill of the pilot is shown in weathering the storm at " least, though he should not gain his port." Public merit (agreeable to the extended view of that great orator and statesman, as expressed afterwards) consists in "having " been inflexible in our intentions for the public welfare, " and not by a positive perseverance in certain favourite " modes of obtaining it."

It will be unnecessary to trace the petty differences which took place between the Commander-in-Chief and the Governor: the general character and evil effect of these differences have been described. The first act which led to serious discussions, was the former placing the Quarter-Master-General, Lieutenant-Colonel Munro, in arrest. The nature of this case is well known: and few, I imagine, can doubt that Government had *a right* to command his release: but it will remain a question with many, how far a knowledge of the character and actual temper of the Commander-in-Chief, the state of the army, and other circumstances, would have warranted Government in forbearing to use *this right*. It is nonsense to say, that it would, by so forbearing and moderate a proceeding, have abandoned an officer entitled to protection. This language, if it means any thing, implies that Government did not conceive there were at that moment thirteen officers, either in the King's or Company's service, on the coast, upon whose honesty and honour it could rely. This is a proposition which appears too extravagant for notice: but, even if this point be conceded, will it be said, if Colonel Munro had suffered an additional injustice by the sentence of a violent and partial court martial, that the

Government was, in that extreme case, deprived of the right to protect that officer ? On the contrary, would not the necessity for the exercise of that right have been, under such an event, much more apparent and unobjectionable. It may be asked, If any circumstances could justify Government in so pusillanimous a conduct, as that of forbearing to exercise an admitted right, and of allowing a court martial to judge upon a public act which it had recognised and approved? It is to be replied, that such conduct might, on many occasions, be the result of prudence and of fortitude. It is weakness, not firmness, that takes an early alarm at danger, and by showing a want of confidence in all the subordinate aids of its power, creates, by its suspicion, that defection which it apprehends. In the recent case of Sir Francis Burdett, the House of Commons did not abandon its exclusive right, but it forbore the exercise of that right, and, with a confidence and wisdom worthy of so enlightened and august an assembly, allowed a question, which involved its rights and authority, to be discussed in a court of law. There can, I should conceive, be no doubt whatever, that had Colonel Munro been tried on the charges preferred against him, he would have been honourably acquitted ; and the influence and reputation of his accusers would have been in no slight degree lessened : an object which, in itself, was of consequence at that period to Government.

It is a remarkable fact, that the officers who had signed the charges against Colonel Munro, were, on reflection, and from learning the sentiments of the Judge-Advocate-General, so convinced that the charges they had made were either groundless or illegal, that they wrote to the Commander-in-Chief to suspend the prosecution of them. This certainly proves (if any proof was wanting) that there could have been no doubt of the result of a court martial, grounded on the state of general feelings, as far as that regarded the charges against Lieutenant-Colonel Munro ; for if the accusers themselves had shown they distrusted the cause they had so rashly adopted, there could, assuredly, be no apprehension of the judgment of thirteen officers of rank (all of whom, if it had been thought necessary, might have been chosen from his Majesty's service) giving a biassed or unjust sentence. The Government of Madras, in their dispatch to the Court of Directors upon this subject, draw a directly opposite conclusion from this fact, which, they say, "proves in itself the inexpediency "of their having had recourse to such a proceeding;" but they state no grounds for this conclusion. In the whole course of this affair they appear to have been much, if not solely, guided by the opinion of their law officers: and no man can peruse the letter of Lieutenant-Colonel Leith upon this subject, without a just respect for the talents and extensive legal knowledge of that public officer. But those that think great, numerous, and obvious evils resulted from the decision of Government on the case of Lieutenant-Colonel Munro, will not immediately perceive the necessity of its having been governed by rules of law in its decision on a question which clearly involved the most serious considerations of state policy. They will think, and with justice, this was a question not for lawyers, but statesmen; who, in the exercise of their legitimate discretion, are in the situation in which Mr. Burke has so well described legislators; and therefore, like them, "ought to do what lawyers cannot, for they have no "rules to bind them but the great principles of reason "and equity and the general sense of mankind; these "they are bound to obey and follow: and rather to "enlarge and enlighten law by the liberality of legislative "reason, than to fetter and bind their high capacity by "the narrow constructions of subordinate artificial jus-"tice."

Several months previous to General McDowall's departure for England, that officer had been called upon by the Governor to repress a Memorial to the Governor General, on the subject of late reductions, which was stated to be in agitation at the principal stations of the army. General M^c^Dowall had written circular letters to forbid such proceedings; and nothing further appeared upon this subject till that officer, on the 23d of January 1809, forwarded and strongly recommended to notice a Memorial to the Honourable the Court of Directors signed by a number of the officers of the army, and containing, in moderate and not disrespectful language, a statement of what they deemed their grievances, which chiefly referred to the equalization of their allowances with the Bengal establishment, the hardship of the several reductions of emolument which they had lately sustained, and the partiality in appointment to commands which they conceived was still shown to his Majesty's officers. General M^c^Dowall forwarded, at the same time, another Memorial, which was also addressed to the Court of Directors, and signed by a number of officers commanding native corps, regarding the injury they conceived they had sustained by the abolition of the tent contract. The principle of both these Memorials was strongly condemned by the Government. The former, they informed the Commander-in-Chief, would be sent to the Governor General in Council; and the latter was returned, as relating to a subject which had already been decided.

There were many circumstances connected with these addresses, which confirm the truth of those sentiments I before expressed regarding the feelings by which General M^c^Dowall allowed himself to be governed at this moment: but the state of his mind, and the operation that was likely to have upon the officers of the army, was a subject that merited the serious consideration of Government; which, unless satisfied that there was no danger from the progress of such a spirit of discontent as then existed, should either have adopted *at that moment* some decided measures to repress that evil, or have carefully avoided every act of aggravation. If both of these Memorials had been merely permitted to go as numbers of the dispatch to England, those by whom they were signed would have thought nothing more of their grievances till an answer was received from the Directors: and that, if contrary to their wishes, would have been deemed final, and the Directors would assuredly not have censured Government for a slight departure from established rules at a period when, from extraordinary events, of a nature never likely to happen again, the army was not only in a state of great agitation, but the civil power had lost the aid of that high military authority on which it would in common times have relied to subdue so dangerous a spirit. Few will contend that there would have been any loss of either dignity or of strength in such a proceeding: and how completely, had it been adopted, would the turbulent and seditious be deprived of one of their chief means of increasing irritation*. But this question appears to have been decided,

* As if an unqualified refusal to forward these Memorials was not adequate to produce this dangerous effect, the names of all the officers who had signed the first Memorial were placed on a proscribed list, and deemed ineligible to any promotion in commands or staff situations. One fact will show the impression that this act made upon the most moderate. I wrote to Colonel Aldwell Taylor, an officer of high rank and respectability, expressing my earnest desire to see him placed in a command in which I thought his principles and character would be useful to Government. In his answer, which is dated the 29th of July, he details the causes of his being in a situation of actual retirement. When he had applied for a command to which his services gave him a right to aspire, he observes, that he was informed of the crime by which he had not only forfeited all hope of that particular station, but also (he adds), "that for having affixed "my signature to a respectful address to my superiors and employers, I "was placed at the head of a list of names comprising nearly two thirds "of the army, and thereby marked by the extreme displeasure of Government, and thence deprived of every future hope of situations of honour "and emolument. Whilst smarting under these most serious injuries, I "felt it impossible to resume the command of Masulipatam, and made "application to retire." This case is more marked than others of the same kind, because there can be little, if any doubt, the violent mutiny that took place at Masulipatam would never have occurred, if Colonel Taylor had remained in command of that garrison. The nature of this unavowed punishment (for though there is, I imagine, no doubt such a

like every other, upon an abstract consideration of its own merits as a single and insulated question; and in that light the decision was *undoubtedly right:* but if it had been viewed, as it certainly should, in its relation to the actual state of the army, *it was as certainly wrong.* It had an evident and malignant action throughout all the troubles that ensued. And this absolute, and, as they deemed it, unnecessary and ungracious refusal to allow their grievances to be even heard by the Court of Directors, combined with the punishment* with which it was accompanied, rankled to the last in the minds of the discontented, and indeed appeared to be one of the few subjects, on the hardship and injustice of which the most moderate of those concerned agreed with the most violent.

The next event of consequence, was the publication of a general order, under date the 28th January, by the Commander-in-Chief, censuring Lieutenant-Colonel Munro for his appeal to the civil Government against his decision; an act which General McDowall deemed destructive of subordination, subversive of discipline, and a violation of (what he termed) the sacred rights of the Commander-in-Chief. There can, I should conceive, be little doubt regarding the character of this order. It is certainly indefensible. It in substance arraigned the exercise of an act of authority, the legality of which General McDowall had recognised by his obedience a few days before, and in this view was highly disrespectful to Government, who were justly incensed at the proceedings; and who, in an order under date the 31st of January, removed General McDowall from the command of the army, which it appeared he had not then resigned, though on his way to

resolution was passed by Government, it was never published in any order,) is very peculiar; but it is very characteristic of the system of measures pursued. It was teasing and aggravating in its operation, without efficiency in its end.

* Vide the preceding note.

Ceylon for the purpose of proceeding to England. The links that bound the cause of General M Dowall to that of the officers of the Company's army on the coast, were neither strong nor durable : a common feeling of discontent against Government had united them for a moment, but there was no cohesion either from similar objects or interests ; and the Government order, as far as related to General McDowall, could have given rise to no serious consequences : but the suspension from the service, in the same order, of Major Boles, the Deputy-Adjutant-General, on the ground of his having given currency to the obnoxious order of the Commander-in-Chief, had an immediate and electric effect over the whole army. There was hardly an officer in either the King's or Company's service that did not doubt the justice of this measure, or that did not feel that it inflicted a vital wound on the first principles of military discipline ; and the universal clamour and indignation that it excited, was no doubt the proximate and direct cause of the rebellion that ensued.

The merits of this unhappy act of power have been fully investigated in England ; and the general opinion seems decidedly against the Government of Fort St. George. The wisdom and expediency of the act is defended by none ; and some of the first law authorities * in England doubt its justice. The subject has been completely exhausted ; and I shall say no more upon it, than that there, perhaps, never was so complete a want of knowledge displayed of the character of military feeling, as in the attempt made to prevail upon Major Boles to degrade himself in his own profession, by making an apology for having performed what he deemed his duty, and what he could not have expressed regret for having done, without an admission of guilt. The urgency with which this apology was sought, is of itself a proof that the Government had been precipitate. How much more manly, wise, and digni-

Vide Mr. Pigott's Opinion, printed with the Memorial of Major Boles.

fied, would it have been to have rescinded the resolution which had been taken, on the plain ground of a conviction that Major Boles had erred from want of knowledge, and without intention of offence; and such must have been the actual sentiments which were entertained of his conduct, or Government could never have professed itself ready to accept a slight apology. But a little stickling spirit about supposed dignity, more worthy of a wrong-headed individual engaged in an affair of honour, than a great Government, prevented this obvious measure, and produced irremediable mischief to the state.

On the 1st of February, the day subsequent to that on which Major Boles was suspended, an order was issued, suspending the Adjutant-General, Lieutenant-Colonel Capper, for the same offence, that of being concerned in circulating the offensive order of the Commander-in-Chief. The only difference in the facts of this case from that of Major Boles, (they were alike in principle), was, that Colonel Capper, the moment he heard of Major Boles's suspension, made a declaration, that the circumstance of his being with General McDowall was the sole cause that had led to Major Boles's name being affixed to orders which it was his (the Adjutant-General's) duty to sign; and that he considered all responsibility connected with the office of Adjutant-General rested solely with him, as principal. The generous object of this gallant and meritorious officer (who was lost on his passage to England), was to exculpate his deputy. He did not, however, succeed in that object; and his free avowal of the principal share he had in the circulation of the order was instantly taken as the ground for inflicting a similar punishment on him.

From the hour that these measures were adopted, the state of the army underwent a complete revolution. The most discontented had, till this period, been cautious in their measures, and aimed at no more than obtaining some attention to what they deemed their grievances. There is no doubt, that before these orders were issued a very general spirit of dissatisfaction prevailed; but there was no danger of that taking any mutinous or rebellious shape. Many, and among these some of the most respectable officers in the army, had up to this date taken no concern in those proceedings that had offended Government: but the suspension of Colonel Capper and Major Boles (particularly the latter, who, it was perfectly known, had no share in the councils of the Commander-in-Chief, and whose act of signing and issuing the obnoxious order was therefore exclusively ministerial,) effected a complete and dangerous change in the general temper. All seemed to be actuated by the same resentment at measures which they deemed arbitrary and unjust; and many officers of the highest rank and first respectability, both in his Majesty's and the Honourable Company's service, joined in reprobating the principle upon which it was adopted. The subsequent efforts made to prevail upon Major Boles to sign an apology, and the letter circulated by the commanding officer of the forces, General Gowdie, which condemned that officer for not having acceded to this proposition, had the double effect of increasing the indignation at Government and the popularity of Major Boles, who was, after this act, deemed an honourable martyr in a cause which it was the duty of every military officer to support. Before the more moderate, and with them all those officers of his Majesty's service who had given way to their first feelings, had recovered from their error, numbers of the more violent in the Company's service were irretrievably pledged to violent and guilty proceedings, into which there is no doubt they were deluded by the force of example, and the assurance that the cause in which they were engaged was general. The first of their acts which attracted the notice of Government, was the agitation and preparation of an address to the Governor General, remonstrating against the acts of the Government of Fort St. George, and soliciting the removal of Sir George Barlow; and an address, or letter, to Major Boles, conveying to that officer a contribution for his support during what the addressers deemed his unjust suspension. The Government, in an order dated the 1st of May, 1809, suspended Captain J. Marshall and Lieutenant-Colonel Martin, on the ground of their being principally concerned in preparing the Memorial * (or, as it is termed in this order, "seditious paper,") addressed to the Governor General; and the same punishment was inflicted upon Lieutenant-Colonel the Honourable Arthur St. Leger, on the ground of his having promoted the circulation of the Memorial in the corps under his command. Major J. de Morgan was suspended for nearly similar reasons. Captain James Grant, commanding the body-guard of the Governor, (but then absent on service in Travancore,) had signed the address to Major Boles; and, from a feeling congenial with his candid and gallant character, he deemed concealment of this act dishonourable, nor could he reconcile to his mind the propriety of continuing to hold his appointment with the line he had pursued. He wrote, therefore, a private letter to Major Barclay, (Military Secretary to the Governor,) stating the reasons that had led him to resign the command of the body-guard, and desiring that Sir George Barlow might be informed of his motives; and he enclosed (that the information of the Governor regarding the actual state of the feeling of the army might be complete,) a copy of the letter to Major Boles. He was suspended on the ground of having signed the address to Major Boles; which document, it was stated in the order, he had forced on the attention of the Governor in Council. Lieutenant-Colonel Robert Bell, the commanding officer of the artillery, was removed from all military charge and command, on the ground (as was stated in the orders,) of his having promoted the circulation of a paper similar in substance (to that address) among the officers under his

* This crude and violent address was never transmitted to the Governor General. The crime laid to the charge of the officers here mentioned, was being implicated in framing it and in promoting its circulation

command. Lieutenant-Colonel Chalmers was removed from his immediate command, on the charge of not having reported to Government, or exerted himself to repress, the exceptionable proceedings of the officers under his orders: and Lieutenant-Colonel Cuppage was removed, on the same ground, from the staff situation of Adjutant-General, to which (though he then held a station of command in Malabar,) he had been appointed: while Captain Coombes was deprived of his staff office of Assistant-Quarter-Master-General in Mysore, on the general grounds of being concerned in these reprehensible proceedings. This order concluded by a panegyric upon the discipline and fidelity which the troops in his Majesty's service had invariably shown, and by a compliment to all those of the Company's service who had not taken a share in these reprehensible proceedings, but particularly the subsidiary force at Hyderabad, the conduct of which was stated to have been most satisfactory and exemplary.

Though the right of suspending officers from the service till the pleasure of the Court of Directors was known, is one that has been very properly vested in the local Governments of India, they possess no power which should be exercised with such extreme caution. It never can be wisely exercised in any cases but those of most clearly established guilt, where trial would either endanger the authority of Government, or expose its dignity to the highest insult and degradation; which is indeed one, and perhaps the most effectual, mode of endangering its existence. Every officer is conscious, when he enters the public service, that he subjects himself to military law, but not to arbitrary power. There are, however, (as has been shown), extreme cases, which create exceptions that interfere with his right to this jurisdiction: but when the ruling power is compelled to act contrary to usage, it is bound, in all such cases, to establish the necessity of its so acting, by an exposure both of the nature of the crime and of the proof of its having been committed*. The King of England may, no doubt, strike any officer's name out of his army without assigning any reason; but his adviser would incur serious responsibility; and an inferior authority exercising this great power should be still more cautious, lest the very purpose for which it was granted be perverted, by the destruction of that general confidence in the justice of their rule, upon which the power of departure (when the safety of the state absolutely requires it) from ordinary forms of law is grounded. No sense of expedience, or desire to strike terror, (by the mere display of arbitrary power,) can warrant the slighest deviation from principles so essential to preserve the temper and order of a military body under this alarming though legal departure from its usual rights and privileges.

It was a remarkable fact, relative to the orders issued on that date, that (unless in the case of Captain Grant, who had come forward to accuse himself † of the act for which he was punished) no proof of the guilt of any of the others was brought forward. They were, indeed, almost all suspended, removed, and disgraced, on the grounds of private information; which, supposing it true, could not, from its nature, and the resentment to which it would expose individuals, be publicly stated. The consequence was, that many of the individuals who had been thus condemned and punished without a hearing, loudly declared their innocence, and brought strong presumptive evidence to support their assertion. They were generally believed; and a sense of their particular wrongs, added to the alarm

* There may be some rare exceptions to this rule, which apply to secret confederacies against a state, where the object is to *deprive an individual of power, more than to punish as an example*. This consideration could, on the 1st of May, have hardly applied even as a fair pretext to any one individual of the many that were punished.

† In this officer's case there was no impropriety or disrespect in the letter, that could have aggravated the offence; and the motive which made him state what he had done, was assuredly honourable.

caused by the sweeping use which Government had on this occasion made of its right of suspending officers without trial, greatly aggravated the discontented, who felt an almost maddening motive to action in the immediate contemplation of the ruin and disgrace which threatened some of the most honourable and distinguished of those that had taken any share in their proceedings.

The obvious and acknowledged source of the crimes which Government had at this moment to punish, was its own act—the recent suspension of Lieutenant-Colonel Capper and Major Boles; and it ought to have been evident, that the orders of the 1st of May would aggravate, in the highest degree, the general agitation which that measure had produced; and almost every paragraph of this order would appear as if intended for that object. The thanks given in it to his Majesty's troops were no doubt merited, but invidious; and, being so, could never have been desired by that body; many of whom, though they had been led (by the operation of the principles of the distinct constitution of the army to which they belonged,) to renounce every share in the proceedings of the discontented officers in the Company's service, still participated in their feelings: but the useless irritation of this part of the order appears a trifling error when compared to that eulogium which it so unfortunately bestowed on the Hyderabad force, whose officers, however much circumstances might have prevented their coming forward, could not possibly, as a body, have a separate interest from the rest of that army to whom they were on this occasion held forth as a corps on whose fidelity Government had peculiar confidence. The operation of such praise was inevitable: the Company's officers at Hyderabad were not only exposed to the reproach of inaction in what were deemed objects of common interest, but to the accusation of being in part the cause of the ruin of some of the most popular officers of the army: for the discontented argued, that if Government had not thought it could rely on their support, it never would have had recourse to so bold and arbitrary a course of measures. Correct information regarding the temper of this force would have satisfied Government that there was no good ground for this eulogium ; and the slightest reflection on the common motives of human action would have prevented its being made. The Company's officers at Hyderabad treated the praise bestowed upon them with scorn, disclaimed all right to it in an address to Government, and, abandoning that moderation which had before characterized their proceedings, they commenced with all the zeal of converts in their new career. In their ardour to make amends for the past, they took the lead in violence. Their numbers and apparent unanimity inspired them with fatal confidence : and this force, who were excited to action by a weak and unwise attempt to divide them from the rest of the army, became the most active promoters of sedition, and gave an example of opposition to Government, in which their repentance came too late to prevent the ruin of many of those who were betrayed, by a reliance on them, into the adoption of the same unjustifiable course.

The general spirit of indignation which the orders of the 1st of May were calculated to excite, must have been foreseen ; but it was perhaps expected, that the terror struck by so decided and vigorous a proceeding would repress the effects of this spirit, and alarm even the most violent into order and obedience. If such was the intention, the measure was certainly inadequate to the end proposed. When we bear in mind the inflamed state of the minds of a great majority of the officers of the coast army, was it reasonable to expect, that the suspension from the service, and the removal from their commands, of a few of the most popular (including some of the most moderate*) officers in the service, would strike a panic in a body of men so agitated ? Was it not more likely that they would

* It is, of course, meant the most moderate among those who were at all discontented.

deem this a repetition of what they had before considered injustice, and rush on the extreme of violence? It could have no other effect; and therefore, if it had been resolved to take no steps to conciliate or restore the temper of the army, this was the period (before their combinations were matured,) that a severe and wise Government would have chosen to come to issue; and, had the danger been fully met at this moment, those consequences which resulted from the line pursued would, in all human probability, have been avoided: but if the object of the Government of Fort St. George had been the ruin of its own army, no measures could have been more calculated to effect that object than those pursued. The character of its acts till the 1st of May has been fully shown. It would be as tedious as useless to dwell upon the many trifling but irritating measures to which it had recourse from that period till the 26th of July. These measures were, if not oppressive, all marked by a spirit of the most provoking suspicion, and never contained one particle of that generous feeling of noble confidence, which, by exalting the character of authority, attaches those that are wavering, reclaims the insubordinate to their duty, and, by giving a motive in which they have a pride, recalls the most guilty to the path of honour and virtue. A bare catalogue of a few of the expedients to which the Government resorted will be sufficient to show the nature of the whole. Some officers were removed from the command of corps, and sent to distant stations, without any reason being assigned; others were insulted, by being ordered away from the Presidency and other places at a few hours' warning, upon the ground of private information regarding their conversation or actions. Leave to visit the Presidency was refused to all officers. An institution of cadets (boys) was dissolved, because they had a quarrel with one of their comrades in consequence of his going to Lady Barlow's ball. A corps was removed to a distant and unpleasant (if not unhealthy) station, because its officers refused to dine with the Governor. But the conduct of the officers of the European regiment at Masulipatam, in consequence of a dispute about a toast at their mess-table, and the measures that precipitated a mutiny in that garrison, (the particulars of which will be stated in my narrative,) forms one of the completest examples of the character of that system of irritation pursued by the Government of Fort St George, during this short but important and eventful period. In viewing this system, we ought not to take any single case, but look at the whole; and we shall find it, as such, fully adequate to the end which it effected, of making a brave and meritorious though mistaken body of men rush upon their own ruin; and of greatly weakening, if not destroying, by its probable operation on the attachment and allegiance of our native army, the most essential of all those principles, on the preservation of which must depend the future safety and existence of our empire in India.

The mutiny which an imprudent measure of Government (the particulars of which will be hereafter stated) brought on at Masulipatam, was one of the first acts of open violence committed by the officers on the coast establishment. As the Governor of Fort St. George thought it might be quelled by means short of coercion, he directed me to proceed to that garrison, in the hope that I should recall the officers to their duty. But his other measures ill accorded with the avowed principles of that conciliatory and moderate proceeding. It had long been reported throughout the army, that Government intended to make such a distribution of the native corps as would place them under the complete check of his majesty's regiments. The alarm, and indeed despair, caused by this report, were excessive and general. The numerous officers of the Company's army who had become engaged in guilty combinations, thought their destruction was certain, and that union and resistance offered the only hope of safety. It might not have been the intention of Government to make such an impression; but is it not clear to the most common understanding which reflects on what had passed, and the actual state of feeling in the army, that this impression must have been produced *? Was it not evident that the mutiny at Masulipatam had been caused by the mere rumour of this intention on the part of Government? and could it be expected by the most weak, or infatuated, that the actual execution of this plan would not produce the same effect in a situation such as Hyderabad, where the spirit of disaffection was more violent, and the power of resistance as great, if not greater. It is hardly possible to make any other conclusion, but that those who advised this measure foresaw the result, and thought that such an act of open disobedience would give the colour of unavoidable necessity to the extreme measures † which they then contemplated. It produced its natural effect—the order

* I heard this plan mentioned by an officer high on the staff, the day before I sailed for Masulipatam, and protested against its principle, as directly contrary to that on which I had been desired to act, and indeed to every effort of conciliation. The Governor, to whom I immediately stated this fact, appeared to me to accord in my opinion; but, a few days after my departure, he was induced to adopt this measure, and to provoke disobedience to authority.

† The following are the sentiments of Colonel Close upon this subject, as expressed in his letter to Major Barclay under date the 24th of July, 1809, and published in the correspondence laid before the House of Commons:

" It is generally admitted as a sound maxim, not to hazard the giving " of an order unless there be a fair ground of presumption that it will be " obeyed. From the apparent circumstances of the time, the orders sent " to Masulipatam were perhaps fairly hazarded; but, after those orders " had been disobeyed, to send orders to Hyderabad for the march of a " battalion, might have been regarded as a measure in some degree " exceptionable. The officers, who have opposed the orders sent for the " purpose, are now more forcibly tied together than before. The " extreme of their proceedings is increased, and their danger and fear " seriously heightened. Their impulse to act is become more violent; " and accordingly the loss to the public cause must be in proportion to " all these augmentations. But this is not all. If the measure of moving " the battalion was meant to be useful, in having an experimental effect, " Hyderabad was assuredly the very place at which the experiment for the march of the 2d battalion of the 10th regiment from Hyderabad to Goa was disobeyed; and the Company's officers at that station forced down a precipice of guilt, at which, in spite of their violent language, they shuddered. This act of open disobedience, accompanied by a violent and seditious paper styled their *Ultimatum**; which they transmitted to the Governor, constituted the immediate grounds upon which Government adopted the extreme measure of the 26th of July, of calling upon all the European officers of the native corps to sign a test of their fidelity, and, on their refusal, of separating the officers from their men.

Though a violent agitation certainly existed at this time throughout almost all ranks of the officers of the Company's army, this agitation had a variety of shades, which it is of importance to consider. Many officers in the Company's service had no share whatever in those proceedings which had met with the disapprobation of Government but these, though they severely condemned the conduct of the disaffected, and regretted their errors, could not but be alive to the character and reputation of the army to which they belonged; they were, of course, anxious for measures that would retrieve the service from that disgrace and ruin with which it was threatened: and it was the natural wish of this class (who were stronger in influence than numbers,) that Government should endeavour to reclaim the discontented to their duty by some act that mixed as much consideration and indulgence

" should not have been made; confusion could not be so hurtful any " where else."

Those who know the delicacy of this superior man will judge, from this extract, what must have been the strength of his feelings upon the subject.

* The trial of Lieutenant-Colonel Innes, and the removal from the general staff of some officers obnoxious to the malecontents, were among the demands in this paper.

for the errors into which they had fallen, with a vigorous exertion of its authority as it was possible to mix, without a sacrifice of its strength and dignity.

The next, and a very principal if not a numerous class, were officers of some rank and influence, who had gradually, and without reflection, involved themselves in proceedings, the scope and extent of which they had never contemplated till they had gone too far to retract. They had persuaded themselves that Government would yield to the representations of the army; and the hope of success, added to the fear of being accused of defection, had hitherto kept them firm to the general cause: but these men, at the period of which I speak, contemplated their situation with affliction and horror; they saw themselves borne away in a tide that they could not resist: they conceived, from a false but imperious sense of honour, which, from a singular but powerful principle of human nature, was felt to be the more binding because at variance with duty, that they were pledged to support the rest; or, more properly speaking, not to abandon them. They were sensible too late of having lost their authority and control over the younger and more violent part of the service, and regretted their proceedings; but at the same time saw, under the rigid course pursued by Government, no safety but in union. This class of men would have rushed to any door that had been opened to their retreat; they would have made a stand on any ground that the clemency or generosity of Government had afforded them; and would not only have reclaimed themselves, but the rest; for they were, generally speaking, of that rank and character who had the chief influence with the troops; and, if extremes had been resorted to, with them on the side of Government, the others must have submitted, as their efforts at resistance would have been quite hopeless. The last and most numerous, though certainly the least powerful party among the officers of the coast army, were those who, unfortunately for its reputation, had the chief management of all the criminal proceedings. This party, which consisted of a few wrong-headed and violent old officers, and almost all the junior part of the service, completely took the lead in their correspondence and deliberative committees; in both of which a very violent and indecent tone of proceeding was adopted; and the authority of commanding officers of corps was apparently suspended by the principle of equality introduced in their proceedings. But this loss of power was more apparent than real; for, though the commanding officers may have had little more influence in the committee than the youngest officers, their military authority (generally speaking) remained, and that must have given them, whenever they had the courage to exert it, a very commanding influence over the whole: and this circumstance establishes what has been before stated, that the most numerous, clamorous, and violent, were in fact the least powerful party in the army, though they have assumed a style in the written documents, as if they were the undisputed and uncontrolled leaders of the whole of the Company's army.

The objects of the different classes of officers were, of course, as various as their feelings. The first could have no wish, but such a settlement as should vindicate the dignity of Government, and, as far as possible, spare the character and reputation of the service. They were too well aware of the nature of those causes that had led the discontented astray, not to hope that every effort might be made to reclaim the misguided; but they were prepared, if such efforts failed, to have acted with a forward and animated zeal in support of lawful authority, and to have contributed their efforts to reduce men who had shown themselves unworthy of kindness and indulgence. The next class that has been described required more aid from the consideration of Government, before they could disentangle themselves from those unfortunate pledges into which they had entered. They felt that, after having proceeded so far, they would have been disgraced if they had, by their retreat, left their associates to be punished. These officers thought they could not abandon the cause before it was at least ascertained none should suffer for what had passed; but they had become fully sensible of the deep guilt in which they were involved: and though many of this class had entered into a pledge to have obtained what was termed a redress of grievances (inclusive of a complete repeal of the orders of the 1st of May), they were not disposed to persevere to the extent of disobedience in the pursuit of this object: and had Government, in addition to an act of amnesty, held out the slightest prospect that the officers of the army would, by an immediate return to good order and duty, acquire a claim upon the clemency and consideration of the Court of Directors, which might operate favourably to those officers who were suspended, and who were the object of their painful solicitude, this class would have used their utmost efforts to reclaim the more turbulent, and, in the event of those efforts failing, have employed all their influence and authority with the troops, to have prevented any injury to the state, from the violence or insanity of the rest.

It is difficult to say what were the objects of the last class among the officers of the coast army. This, it has been stated, were the most numerous and most violent, but the least powerful; though it was probably judged otherwise by Government, from this party having throughout conducted the proceedings of the committees, and correspondence, and having always exaggerated its means, and assumed, from a desire to intimidate, a tone as if it spoke the sentiments of all the officers of the army.

One of the earliest motives to action with this class, was a personal hatred of Sir George Barlow*, and of some

* Lord Minto has, in his letter to the secret committee, noticed this feeling, as forming a strong and operative principle of action in the minds of these infatuated men.

officers on the general staff who were supposed to be his chief advisers. This feeling had latterly absorbed every other. From indulging it, they persuaded themselves that they were compelled to the indefensible extremes they had adopted, and thus found an alleviation of that misery in which a sense of guilt had involved them. It would be difficult to state the objects which men acting under the dominion of such passions had in view. They, in fact, did not well know themselves what they desired: but there were, I believe, very few among this class even, so completely unreasonable, as to approve of that paper called *the Ultimatum*, which the officers of the Hyderabad force had the presumption to send to Government.

Such was the diversified temper of the numerous officers of the Company's army on the coast when the test was proposed for universal subscription. In describing that measure, it is perhaps more essential to attend to the mode in which it was carried into execution, than its substance. The Government of Fort St. George had, in consequence of the information which I gave them from Masulipatam *, assembled a field force near Madras. The majority of this camp was formed of his Majesty's troops: but the senior officers of the Company's troops, who composed a part of this corps, were men of whose violence, in whatever situation they were placed, Government could entertain no apprehension †; and every thing might have been expected, under the slightest management, from their good sense and moderation. Sir George Barlow, it is true, sent for some of these officers, and appeared to treat them with confidence in some discussions he had with them on the state of the army: but one fact will suffice to show the character of this confidence, and

* Vide Appendix.

† The names of the principal of these officers, Colonel Clarke, Colonel Rumley, Colonel Floyer, Major Russel, and Captain Noble, will be received by all parties as full evidence of the truth of this assertion.

the general impressions which his conduct on this occasion was likely to make. Lieutenant-Colonel Rumley (who commanded the native cavalry at the Mount, and was one of those respectable officers who were honoured with his confidence,) received, during this period, an extraordinary communication from Major Russel, of an attempt to excite the native officers of the cavalry against their European commanders. It appears of importance to insert this written report, as drawn up by the Major himself. It is as follows:

" On the afternoon of the 23d ultimo *, Secunder Khan " Subahdar came to me, on my return from Madras to " camp, and said he had been very anxious to see me for " several hours, as something of a very extraordinary " nature had occurred. That walking in the vicinity of " the lines he had been accosted by a brahmin, who asked " him if he was not the senior officer of cavalry, and said " he had business of the greatest importance to communi- " cate to him. He then proceeded to disclose to him, " that he had been sent by Colonel Munro to inform the " native troops that their officers had sent in a petition to " Sir George Barlow to be put on Bengal allowances, " which Sir George had informed them the resources of " this country would not admit; and, in consequence of " this refusal, they had resolved to mutiny: that in case " the officers should propose to engage them in seizing " the person of Sir George, it was their duty to say he " was their Governor, and that they would not act in such " a cause. The only way, *he further said, in which the " demand of the officers could be complied with, was by " taking away a proportion of the pay of the native " officers and men.* That if Secunder Khan would under- " take to persuade all the men and officers to act in this " manner, he should receive a handsome jagheer: and " he was further informed, that Colonel Munro had dis-

* July, 1809.

"patched emissaries or letters to communicate the same "to all the native corps in the army. That he had no "occasion to apprehend injury from any one, as he might "observe Sir George had suspended every person who "acted in opposition to his wishes*."

Colonel Rumley was naturally indignant at a proceeding which he was convinced (from the whole behaviour of Sir George Barlow) could not have his sanction, and which he deemed, at the moment, to be an impolitic and dangerous expedient of a person who, enjoying a large share of his confidence, might have acted on this occasion without his knowledge. With these impressions, he hastened to give full information of the circumstance to Sir George Barlow; but his report was received without either emotion or surprise; and he was forced to conclude, from no notice being taken of it, that the measure of which he complained had been adopted by authority. The circumstance became public after Colonel Rumley returned to camp, and the minds of most of the officers were greatly inflamed at this glaring instance of what they deemed unmanly duplicity.

A short account of the mode in which the test was proposed to the officers at Fort St. George and the camp near the Mount, will convey, better than any general detail, the character of the measure. The following is a copy of that remarkable document:—

"We, the undersigned officers of the Honourable Com-"pany's service, do in the most solemn manner declare, "upon our word and honour † as British officers, that we

* Emissaries of a similar character were at and before this period sent to all the native corps.

† Government could not have supposed men very deep in guilt, upon whose solemn assurance that they would fulfil the obligation of their commissions such reliance was to be placed. It was evident, that had they cherished any serious designs against their country, or any of its constituted authorities, they would not have hazarded the failure of their schemes by stickling at the little additional guilt that would have attended the breach of any test so forced upon their acceptance; they

"will obey the orders and support the authority of the "Honourable the Governor in Council of Fort St. George, "agreeable to the tenor of the commission which we hold "from that Government."

This test was sent to the commanding officer of the forces assembled at Fort St. George and the Mount, and it was accompanied by a circular letter to the commanding officers of divisions, which was read to the officers of the Company's service before their signature was required.

The substance of this letter was an order to assemble the Company's officers at each station, to propose the test to them, and instantly to remove from their corps all such as declined to sign it. They were directed to be sent to such stations as the commanding officer chose, and that they should there receive their allowances until the situation of affairs and the temper of their minds should admit of their being employed with advantage to the state.

This was, it must be recollected, the first public appeal that had been made to the officers of the Company's service by the Government of Madras since the orders of the 1st of May; and it certainly was not of a character calculated to flatter the feelings of those to whom it was addressed. It spoke to their sense of duty, and pride as officers; but in the same breath told them they were not trusted, and that they were to be coerced into order and submission. The high praises that were given in this letter to the fidelity and loyalty of his Majesty's troops were perfectly just; but quite unnecessary, as far as regarded the allegiance and obedience of that part of the service; and could there-

would have signed, and watched the opportunity of accomplishing their plans. But of this there was no apprehension: they were acknowledged, at the moment this pledge was presented, to be men of honour, and alive to all the obligations that word implies. And can it be argued that men, with such feelings, were not to be fixed in their duty, or reclaimed to it, by other means than such as *almost imposed opposition as a point of honour*, as by it only they could avoid the reproach of having been trepanned, alarmed, and coerced into a promise to perform that duty which they owed to the state they served.

fore serve no purpose but to exasperate the feelings of the officers of the Company's army. But the mode in which this measure was carried into execution was the most characteristic of the Government by whom it was adopted, and of itself was sufficient to account for its complete failure, and indeed to make it very doubtful if it ever was wished or intended that it should succeed.

No previous effort whatever was made to dispose the minds of the senior and more reflecting part of the Company's officers in favour of this measure, though such a step (which could have been adopted in many ways without the slightest hazard) seemed essential to its success. A short and peremptory summons was sent to every Company's officer of the garrison of Fort St. George, to attend at the quarters of Colonel Conran, the commanding officer. That officer read the circular letter to which I have alluded to the astonished officers whom he had assembled; and then, presenting the test, informed them they must either sign immediately, or go to Pulicat, the place fixed for their banishment. Can any man the least acquainted with the human mind be surprised, that an almost general and indignant rejection was the result of such a proceeding? Five regimental officers only could be prevailed upon to sign it at this meeting; and the remainder were immediately sent to Pulicat*. At the Mount the rejection was still more general. Colonel Hare had the day before removed his tents across the bridge of Marmalon, where all the officers were summoned at an equally short notice. When Colonel Hare read the circular letter, presented the test for signature, and told them that those who refused their signature would not be allowed to return to camp, they refused with one general sentiment of indignation at

* Captain Moodie, the commanding officer, and almost all the officers of the first battalion of the 6th regiment, were among this number, though that corps had, up to this date, been remarkable for never having joined in any one of the guilty or objectionable measures of the army. It was a sense of their past conduct that made such treatment more insufferable.

the manner in which they had been treated, and were immediately separated from their corps*

The test was signed by all the staff-officers at the Presidency, and by some officers who were there on leave; at Trichinopoly twenty-two signed it, but few others at any other station of the army. In short, the whole number of signatures did not amount to one hundred out of about one thousand two hundred, which is near the number of officers on the coast establishment in India.

The almost total failure of this expedient (if it ever was intended to reclaim or fix any officers in the Company's service to their duty,) will not surprise any man the least acquainted with human nature, and with the temper of those to whom the measure was proposed. Those officers, who had never departed from their duty in thought, word, or deed, felt this test, which was a mere repetition of the obligation of their commission, as at least an act of supererogation; and it was painful, as it had a taint of suspicion in it. Others, who were in some degree pledged to support their brother officers, conceived that this was an indirect mode of obtaining their individual pledges to act against them; and concluded, from its being proposed, that every hope of an amnesty was at an end †; whilst the more violent only saw in it the pursuit of plans which banished every expectation from their minds of obtaining

* The senior Company's officer at this meeting was Colonel Clarke, commanding the artillery, who was known to be exempt even from suspicion of any share whatever in the violent proceedings of a part of the army, and had been recently selected on that ground to command at the Mount. Was it not natural that a sense of his own conduct should have led this honourable officer to reject with indignation a proposition made in a mode so insulting to his feelings as a man and an officer.

† To many of this class it must have been an agreeable release from the rigid obligations of their commission. It offered a temporary retirement from their duty to the state; and, in doing so, changed in some degree the *character of that duty*. By signing the test they became volunteers against men whose guilt they had to a certain extent shared, and had no longer, to support their minds in so trying a situation, that plea of indispensable necessity which their commission imposed.

personal security, much less the object they had in view, through any means but successful resistance.

The most moderate among these officers argued, that no opportunity whatever had been given to the Company's army of retrieving itself; and, guilty as it might have been, they said the memory of its former fame merited some consideration; and an appeal to its loyalty and duty, combined with an act of amnesty, would, they thought, if it had been made to the officers of the Company's army with that confidence which inspires attachment, have secured the fidelity of a great part of them: and if it had been possible for Government to have gone further, and to have promised, "that in the event of the conduct of the "army meriting such favour, they would recommend the "case of the officers who had been suspended to the in-"dulgent consideration of the Court of Directors*," they were confident all would have been reclaimed to their duty. But had efforts so worthy, in their opinion, of the clemency and greatness of Government failed in bringing all to reason, they would have acted with the most ardent zeal against men whom they should in such event not only have considered as rebels to their country, but as destroyers of the reputation of the army to which they belonged. There can be no doubt these were the sentiments of many respectable officers of rank and influence: and had Government adopted, on the 26th of July, any such measures of conciliation, it would have been completely successful; and not only the hazard of a contest, but all those disastrous consequences which were certain to be the inevitable consequence of complete success, would have been avoided. And can there be a doubt in the mind of any rational being but it might have taken such a line, at the very moment that which has been described was adopted, without any

* This was the substance of the order that I recommended to be issued at this period, the principle of which has been so arraigned by the Government of Fort St. George. A copy of this order is inserted in the Appendix.

substantial sacrifice of either its strength or dignity, and certainly with the greatest benefit to the interests of the British nation in India?

The measure that was taken was supposed, by almost all the discontented, to be a completion of that design which the Government of Fort St. George had from the first (they conceived) entertained, of relying solely on the King's troops; and they concluded, from the substance as well as the mode in which the step taken on the 26th of July was carried into execution, that the Company's military establishment on the coast was meant to be destroyed at the first blow; and all were therefore included in one general mass, as fit objects of suspicion and disgrace.

Government had, no doubt, a right to expect success in the execution of this measure; it had a just reliance on the fidelity and attachment of his Majesty's troops: A few regiments, who composed part of the British army, could not have joined in such a confederacy without incurring certain and indelible disgrace: and it had been the policy of the Government of Fort St. George, from the first appearance of dissatisfaction and discontent, to court the allegiance and flatter the feelings of this branch of the service. And though no man can calculate the temper that was lost, or the consequent evils that have been produced by this proceeding, the limited object was undoubtedly attained.

Sir George Barlow appears to have had great confidence in the attachment of the native troops to Government; which, I believe, he always thought was paramount to their attachment to their European officers: and this was consequently calculated upon as one great means of carrying his measures into prompt and successful execution: but certainly the fulfilment of this hope depended upon the course pursued by the European officers who commanded these men. There could be no ground to make such a conclusion upon any general principles applicable to military bodies, and much less so from the constitution, character, or history of the native branch of the military establishment in India. The difficulty that a body of officers have in any service, is to keep soldiers to their duty: there is little in debauching them from it. They are led by example: and to follow that of their officers, is both a principle and a habit. The native troops of India are perhaps more attached to their European officers than any others. These officers are to them the only representatives they know of the Government they serve; they are the sole link in the chain of their attachment; and, with rare exceptions, their men are completely devoted to them The Governor might, perhaps, expect, that though this feeling would operate in the first instance, it would soon give way to a fear of losing all those solid benefits that the service of the Company offers; and that the sepoys would never contimue to attach their fortunes to so desperate a cause as that of the officers must soon appear. This is a natural conduct for a sensible and reflecting man: but do soldiers think, or reflect deeply? Would not the increased pay which their officers (if they were serious in rebellion) would be likely to give, or, what is still more attractive to men like them, a latitude to plunder, have more effect than twenty proclamations to recall them to their duty. Besides, had this dreadful contest continued, the passions would have had their way, and a few months might have changed the character of our native soldiery, and rendered them more formidable than all the enemies we ever had to encounter in India.

It will at least appear, from what has been said on the subject, that Government had no right to look to the fidelity and attachment of the native troops, as a certain means of coercing their European officers to obedience: But the fact was, that the sure ground of success, and that on which the Government had more right to calculate (when it resorted to extremes,) than all others put together, was the action of the virtuous feelings and loyal principles of the Company's officers themselves, and the total want of object, accord and combination, in the execution of the indigested plans of the most violent. It was well known that many of those officers had never brought their minds to contemplate disobedience to the state: and the most guilty even, at first proceeded on the idea that such an extreme would never occur. They certainly had hoped that Government would yield, to avoid it: and when they latterly found that result was not likely, they shuddered at the crisis which they had precipitated. They had no object in view that could justify to their own minds the extremes in which they were involved; they found themselves on the point of being placed in the situation of rebels, with minds altogether unsuited to act that part which can alone give a hope of success to the cause of rebellion. They could not (violent as they were against the Governor of Madras and some others) bring their minds to believe they were enemies to a revered King and beloved country; and they consequently wished to reconcile the incompatible principles of opposition to the local Government, with a spirit of fidelity to their employers, and loyalty to their sovereign. There could be no doubt of their sincerity in these feelings: and, from the clashing of such opposite principles of action, Government had a right to expect irresolution, division, and distraction in their councils and measures. It was certain that many would not join in any act of disobedience, and that those who ventured on opposition would proceed with alarm, and every moment of reflection would make them view with increased horror the guilt in which they were involved, and produce a wavering and hesitation that must soon have the effect of losing them the confidence of their followers and of each other.

Under such circumstances, there could be little doubt of the ultimate success of Government in the measures adopted for subduing the refractory European officers of the army. We shall now examine the dangers by which these measures were likely to be attended. These were numerous, and all of an alarming political magnitude*. The greatest, was the shock which was given by this proceeding to that attachment between the European officer and the natives under his command, which, from the first establishment of the Company in India to the present moment, had been looked upon as one of the principal, if not the chief, sources of our strength in India. This body of officers has been hitherto justly considered as the great means by which British India was conquered, and by whose fidelity, knowledge and courage, it was to be maintained. They were comparatively a few persons, through whom a large foreign army was not only disciplined, but attached to the present state. Their station was one of more than ordinary trust, their duties very sacred, and they had for a long period of years been distinguished by the manner in which these had been performed. A part

I might fill a volume if I were to enter into any general reasoning on the vital wound given to military subordination by this measure. The relation of the private soldier to the subaltern has been well termed the key-stone of the arch: an army may survive any other change; but to disturb that relation, is to dissolve the whole: here begins the obedience of the many to the few In civil society, this problem appears of difficult solution: but there, it is the obedience of the dispersed and disarmed many; it is rare, and in well regulated communities almost unfelt. In military bodies it is the hourly obedience, even to death, of the armed and embodied many. The higher links which bind subalterns to their superiors, and these to one chief, are only the obedience of the few to the fewer, and these fewer to one. These relations are easily intelligible. Honour, and obvious interest, are sufficient to account for these: and any injury they sustain can be repaired. But the obedience of the whole body of soldiers to their immediate officers, is that which forms an army, and cannot be disturbed without the utmost danger of total destruction. It was upon this act of the French Assembly that Burke observed, "They "have begun by a most terrible operation; they have touched the central "point, about which particles that compose armies are at repose; they "have destroyed the principle of obedience in the great essential critical "link between the officer and the soldier, just where the chain of military "subordination commences, and on which the whole of that system de-"pends." Sir George Barlow, it has been forcibly remarked, could discover no other mode of suppressing a *rebellion* of officers than by exciting a *mutiny* of *soldiers*.

of them had been seduced, and misled into error, an ultimately hurried away, by their passion and resentment against individuals in authority, to the most criminal extremes. They certainly had merited, in the strictness of military law, the most serious punishment; and it was, no doubt, as far as the principles of that law were concerned, most desirable, for the sake of example, that punishment should be inflicted, particularly as those officers had in this instance endeavoured to pervert that complete obedience which their men owed them, into an engine of faction and revolt; and to render the attachment of those under their command, which had been so long considered the safety of their country, its future bane and danger. That any body of officers should have, or conceive they had, the power of furthering their own views or interests by means so desperate, and so entirely subversive of the foundations of all order and government, was, no doubt, an evil of great magnitude: but it should have been recollected, that the connexion between the native soldiers and their European officers is the cherished plant of a hundred years: and before we can account those men wise who laid the axe to its trunk, it must be proved that the existing spirit of insubordination among the European officers was attended with dangers as imminent and as incapable of remedy, as the evil that has been embraced by the deliberate dissolution of this great bond of our strength and safety. Some persons, who refer to a former occasion* on which the Indian army are supposed in some degree to have overawed the Government into a redress of their grievances, and viewing only one side of this great question, may argue, that it was rather desirable to adopt a measure that would prevent the European officers from having such reliance on the support of their men, and teach the latter that they have a duty paramount even to their obedience to their officers, in that which they owe the state: but it is a great

* 1794 and 1795.

fallacy to conceive that such a feeling can ever exist as an operative principle in the minds of such a class of men; and if it did, it must weaken a devotion and attachment that are quite essential to the preservation of our power in India*

The next positive evil that was certain to attend this course of measure, was the destruction of that harmony which it had been the labour of years to introduce and maintain between his Majesty's and the Company's service, and which had so greatly contributed to our military successes in India. It could hardly be expected that these would (for some years at least) serve together again with those sentiments towards each other which before inspired them: and nothing can be so dangerous to our interests in India, as feelings of irritation and jealousy being kindled betwixt the two services. Those who have cast away this harmony, which has so long been deemed one of the chief sources of our permanent strength, would perhaps see more security to the Government of India in an irreconcileable division between the King's and Company's troops. But there is no danger of an error, in predicting that the date of our rule over India will be short, if our Government in that quarter can only be supported by such weak and wretched expedients as that of keeping up a principle of division among its own officers.

The last positive and immediate evil which could not but attend this measure, was that effect which it was calculated to produce among the natives of all ranks and

* There can be no doubt of the truth of the observation which a great and well-informed statesman formerly made upon this question. "The European character in India" (Lord Melville observes in one of his letters to the Court of Directors) "cannot be raised too high. If the natives "should be accustomed to look upon persons in the British service with "indifference and contempt, they will rapidly annihilate our Empire "there, and with it the very few Europeans by whom that country is "held in subjection." If this is true of Europeans in general, and our Indian subjects, with what particular force must it apply to the relations between the sepoy and his European commander?

classes. Our strength in India has hitherto greatly rested upon the supposed impossibility of any civil commotion among ourselves: and the dissolution of this charm will give rise to a thousand doubts regarding the stability of our power; and, in all human probability, excite ambitious projects to assail it. This effect is of a magnitude that in itself required every exertion should be made to avoid an extreme that could not but make so general and dangerous an impression regarding the character of our power in India. It must show our enemies in that quarter that we are not exempt (as it has long been believed we were) from those internal divisions and civil wars which have accelerated the fate of the other conquerors of the East*.

There is one more consideration connected with this question. The comparative safety which appeared in the gradual removal of those radical causes which created a spirit of discontent, over a system of harsh coercion under the most unfavourable circumstances that could be supposed, whether we consider the situation of Government or the army. It is not necessary in this place to detail all those

* The most violent even among the officers were so alarmed at the evil this impression must produce to their country, that they carefully avoided, till the last extremity, any mention of it to the natives under their command: not, I am satisfied, from any fear of failing in their efforts to debauch them from their duty, but from a deep sense of the danger of such a communication: and those who believe that the defeat of this confederacy through the means adopted will for ever prevent the occurrence of a similar evil, should recollect, that it is just as likely to have an opposite effect, and to render that evil, if brought on by similar causes, far more dangerous. The European officers may, in their next quarrel with their local Government, be taught by this failure to league with the native officers, and to hold out advantages to them that will secure their most zealous co-operation; and such a conspiracy would lose India. It is dangerous even to hold an opinion that this Empire can be preserved by any means but the action of a wise, temperate, and just Government, which, though firm and powerful, must rule its British subjects with the greatest attention to those habits and principles which are, from the form and character of the constitution under which they are born, inherent in their nature, and which can never be disregarded or offended without a danger of sedition or convulsion.

causes. One of them, which excited great discontent (though certainly not rebellion), was undoubtedly that system of reduction which at this time threatened to leave the Company's officers in India without a motive of action. They saw (at the period of its progress) no prospect of any alteration in their condition that would, by elevating the service and facilitating their return to their native country, make amends for what they lost; and their minds gave way to greater despair, from an impression that those who *they believed* were founding their fortune and reputation on the reduction of their allowances, took no interest in obtaining any advantages to counterbalance what was taken from them. This grievance, unallayed by a hope of redress, had an effect upon the general temper of the army that merited the greatest attention.

But the fact is, the Government of Fort St. George never appear to have taken any view of this subject, that comprehended those considerations which have been stated. They seem to have decided every question, as it arose, upon its own narrow ground, and to have always been fettered in the forms of their own proceedings*. The order for the imposition of the test which was pre-

* As a proof of this, the following fact will suffice. At the period the test was promulgated, a direct correspondence, in the native language, was opened by the chief civil and military officers of Government with the native officers. This was equally maintained with those corps, the European officers of whom remained firm in their duty, as others; and a respectable Company's officer, who had signed the test, and was commanding a corps at Madras, (on his senior subahdar bringing him letters of this description, which he had received,) made a representation of the circumstance; but was reprimanded for doing so, and told it was a general rule, from which it was not deemed proper to make any deviation. If it had been desirable to make any communications in the native languages to the men, such could assuredly have been forwarded to the European officer in command, and the principles of military discipline observed; but an observance of the general rule was the point to which *importance was attached*, even in a case where the operation was *admitted* to be baneful, and consequently where the more *limited* that was, the better for the public interests.

scribed to the Company's officers, was positive, and vested no discretion. In stations where the superiority of his Majesty's troops was decided, this character of the order could do no mischief: but few of those acquainted with the circumstances can doubt, that to the wisdom and forbearance of Lieutenant-Colonel the Honourable Patrick Stuart, of his Majesty's 19th regiment, who took upon himself to suspend the execution of this positive order, and to give time for the action of reason upon minds under the sole dominion of passion, may be attributed not only the safety of that corps, but the tranquillity of Travancore: A similar conduct was observed by Lieutenant-Colonel Forbes, of his Majesty's 80th regiment, who commanded in Malabar; and by Colonel Gibbs, of the 59th regiment, at Bangalore: and the evidence of these respectable officers must be conclusive with regard to the actual temper of the Company's officers under their command, on the day they received the orders of the 26th July, and prove to the most incredulous, how easily men under the influence of such feelings as they describe, might have been reclaimed by means far short of that baneful measure which was adopted.

The force at Hyderabad continued but a short period in a state of resistance; and they committed no act of violence. The impression which Colonel Close's effort (though unsuccessful at the moment) had made upon both the minds of European officers and natives, the effect produced by the perusal of an order issued by Lord Minto on the 20th of July, and the knowledge that his lordship was hourly expected at Madras, deprived rebellion of its chief motive —personal hatred to Sir George Barlow. And these circumstances, aided by the unremitted conciliatory efforts of the commanding officer, Colonel Montresor, and the Resident, Captain Sydenham, made a complete change in the sentiments of this corps, who upon the 12th of August signed the test: and as their example encouraged many corps of the army, but particularly those that formed the garrison of Seringapatam, in a rebellious resistance to Government, their defection from the cause put an end to this horrid and unnatural contest: and Lord Minto, who arrived a few days after this event, found a complete and unreserved submission to his authority. Had he arrived a month earlier, he would have saved an army from disgrace and ruin: and as it was, it is not easy to calculate the good which his presence effected: but it is not unreasonable to conclude, that the report even of his approach went farther to terminate the partial rebellion that had occurred, than all the violence of the Madras Government.

The whole of these proceedings ought to be held in constant remembrance by all parties in future times. "As "they have existed for our shame, they ought to exist for "our instruction *."

To the officers of the Indian army they are awfully instructive. They will not consider a few remarks on the nature of that instruction as unbecoming in one who has served with them for near twenty-eight years; who came among them in childhood; whose fortune and character have been acquired with them; whose affection and pride are, and always must be, deeply interested in their reputation.

If they dispassionately consider these events, they will clearly perceive the danger of the first approaches towards a military combination, intended only to solicit a Government, but necessarily tending to influence, to overawe, and to coerce it. The purity of intention affords no security against this progress. Men who deliberate and confederate with arms in their hands soon become impatient of the slow course of redress by regular means. Indignant at refusals, or even delays, which they deem unjust, they become familiar with the dangerous idea of seeking more summary justice. They assemble, their passions are kindled by communication of grievances, they are emboldened by a

* Burke.

sense of collective strength, and proceed from solicitations to threats, disguised (from the great majority of those that use them) in the form of predictions apparently flowing from an anxious desire to avert the evils foretold.

Such addresses bring upon them censure and harsh imputation, which they resent the more because they are not yet distinctly conscious of intentions which merit them. Their language becomes still more indecorous and violent; and some of their most conspicuous leaders are punished. They have then unhappily placed themselves in a situation where they are pushed forward on the road of guilt by the most virtuous impulses of the human heart—fidelity towards each other, honourable attachment to the distinguished members of their body become sufferers in their cause, and indignation against what they (under the influence of self-delusion) regard as insupportable tyranny, impel them onward with irresistible force. Youth with all its generous feelings, its inexperience and its impetuosity, assumes the lead in their councils. The prudent and the moderate are either banished as traitors, or compelled to be instruments of the more inconsiderate and daring. They find that they have forfeited all expectation of a tolerable pardon. They see no hopes of safety but in victory; and they are hurried on by fear and despair, as well as anger and resentment, to rebellion.

Thus terminates in guilt the progress of men who began with innocence and honour; and of whom each, if the termination had been foretold even when he was far advanced in impropriety, might with sincerity have exclaimed, "*Is* "*thy servant a dog, that he should do this great thing?*"

Any event of such a rebellion would be most unfortunate to those engaged in it, but success would be the greater misfortune, and indeed the most severe punishment with which the justice of Providence could visit their guilt

Success would every where be a dreadful calamity to a body of British officers betrayed into military rebellion against the civil authorities of their country. Their success would be the destruction of every source and guard of their own security, and of every thing of which the defence peculiarly ennobles and endears the profession of arms to a British soldier. In India, however, this misfortune of success would have very bitter aggravations. As soon as British officers had oppressed the lawful authority, they would quickly discover what, in the tumult of dissension, their passions had concealed from them, that they had, though unknowingly, raised their arms against their country, which must espouse the cause of her delegated authorities*. They would thus be proscribed and exiled by a country, the hope of revisiting which is the basis of every plan and expectation of their lives.

Apprehending mutiny among their soldiers, revolt among their subjects, irruption from their Asiatic neighbours, or conquest by some European state, no longer guarded by their own country, but the objects of her just hostility, they would find themselves alone and unprotected in the world. In this friendless situation they could be supported by no generous enthusiasm, the child of patriotism and honour, which could awaken no feeling in their bosom but shame and remorse. Their numbers could only be kept up by adventurers, the refuse of the military profession in Europe. The civil wars, inevitable in such a state of things, would be not so much the consummation of their evils, as a refuge from such intolerable calamities.

Happily for the British officers in India, (I speak not paradoxically, but considerately,) no such calamity is pro-

* These are not sentiments formed on a contemplation of the result of the disturbances. I presented a similar picture of their situation to the deluded officers at Masulipatam, and circulated a letter containing all the substance of these reflections to the army previous to the occurrence of any deliberate opposition to Government. Vide Appendix: Letter to Lieutenant-Colonel McLeod.

bable. They are sure of being haunted by so many "compunctious visitings of nature," from the thoughts of their friends, of their Sovereign, of their beloved country, as to impair that criminal energy necessary for the success of desperate enterprizes. Their's is not a country, or a state of manners, or a system of religion and morality, which trains men to revolutionary sternness and ferocity. Their failure was, and ever will be, certain. But such convulsions bring dreadful consequences :—the loss of that collective character which was the source of pride to each individual, long regret and remorse, their hearts taught to dread generous and social feeling ; and the most distinguished of them, if not condemned to death, still more unhappily abandoned to a dishonourable life.

In their native land they will meet little or none of that sympathy which supports the sufferers for a general cause. Their discontent appears to spring only from the most ignoble sources. Those who have not visited India will not easily conceive that a pecuniary retrenchment is chiefly felt *(which it really is)* as a degradation, by an army already sufficiently excluded from the higher rewards of valour : first shut out from military honours, and then from that compensation for them which they had found in the prospect of returning home to the exercise of generous virtue. Last, and worst of all, they find that their more glaring and dangerous guilt has almost effaced the remembrance of that misconduct which produced it, and given popularity and character to those they deem their enemies.

To the British Governments of India these deplorable occurrences are not less fertile in instruction. They will learn, that to preserve the obedience of a military body, exiled almost for life in a distant dependency, to civil bodies who are the temporary delegates of a Commercial Company, is one of the most difficult problems of policy : that such obedience is not always to be preserved by a rigid adherence to official rules, nor restored by undistinguishing obstinacy clothed in the garb of firmness. They will be taught by high authority, " *how much ought to be* " *done to avert a contest in which concession does not find* " *its place**:"

They will feel, that the difficulty of their policy respecting the army will always be increased at moments when the necessities of the state require extensive retrenchments. A wise Government will prepare the way for such retrenchments, by evidently showing that they are necessary, and that they are equitably imposed on all classes: they will not disdain more particularly to satisfy those distinguished members of an army, whose influence over their brethren is a principle of natural discipline. They will redouble their vigilance to distribute military honours and rewards with the strictest equity; and they will be solicitous to display the appearance as well as the reality of kindness towards the individuals of a body who are about to suffer.

When the passions of the moment have subsided, no man will believe that a Governor, confessedly unpopular†, introducing or maintaining systems of retrenchment, necessary indeed, but most severe, and without preparation, without public precaution or private conciliation, did not, by these circumstances, most materially contribute to the unhappy crisis which followed. The total omission of all those means which make reformation popular, or even tolerable, will assuredly be regarded as a great political offence It will be considered as ridiculous to call for particular proof that a cold and unfeeling manner tended to make privations be felt as insults. No man of common sense will doubt that a popular Governor may reconcile men to retrenchments, which, under a Governor of an opposite character, may produce the most fatal effects. A recent example might be found at no great distance from Madras, (if any examples of what is so obvious were

* Lord Minto. † Vide Lord Minto's dispatch.

necessary,) of a Governor * who had imposed greater retrenchments than Sir George Barlow, and who, without any sacrifice of dignity, left his government, universally beloved. But it will not be doubted that the Government of Madras thus contributed their share towards maturing the discontents of the army previous to the orders of General McDowall. Still less can it be doubted, that by the suspension of Colonel Capper and Major Boles the spark was struck out which fell on the combustible materials.

In the circumstances of the case, and after the restoration of the surviving officer by his superiors, it is very mild language to call this suspension an act of very doubtful justice. And it is most certain, that an act of authority so harsh, and of such doubtful justice, against officers who had such a fair appearance of mere military obedience, and whose very fault, if they had one, must have sprung from a zeal for military privileges, was of a nature to vibrate through every nerve of an army. When the Government once did an act which made two officers of rank at least appear to suffer unjustly for the army, they entirely changed the character of the disputes. They drove the generosity, honour, and justice of the army into rebellion. They supplied the discontented with the colour of right, without which no leaders are ever able to seduce multitudes to resistance. They exalted pecuniary grievances into the feelings of generous sympathy and wounded honour. They made it be thought disgraceful to abstain from taking a part in a combination to prevent injustice. The moderate, the disinterested, the loyal, even the timid and circumspect, were forced into opposition,—by shame, by fear, by sympathy, by that tumultuous combination of causes, generous and mean, which recruit the ranks of insurgents, and change the murmurs of a few into the mutinous clamour of the many. Whatever the evil in-

* General Maitland, late Governor of Ceylon.

tentions of a few may be, it is always an act of real or supposed injustice which throws the multitude into the hands of the ill-affected leaders. Before the suspension there existed only discontents; after it, general disaffection, conspiracy, and sedition.

The necessity of vesting the power of dismissing or suspending officers in the Government will never be questioned by thinking men: but when it is considered, that the operation of the general orders of the 1st of May was, considering the rank and number of the suspended officers, not a much less exertion of authority than if his Majesty were to strike a tenth part of his general officers out of the list of the army, it will not be wondered that this example of the precarious and degraded tenure by which military rank was held, should have diffused universal dismay, and reinforced resentment by despair.

The dispassionate observer, after remarking with wonder that every expedient was omitted or rejected which could detach the misguided from the ill-affected, or open a creditable retreat for the penitent, will pause before the sword was drawn, to consider whether general submission would then have been too dearly purchased by an amnesty which should not have excluded from hope even the officers suspended on the 1st of May.

It will be acknowledged, that the example of a sedition proceeding so far without punishment, is an evil: but it was to be balanced against other evils;—against the calamities of civil war; against the mischief of rendering one part of our military force in India the enemies of the other; against the evils of a victory which must be gained over the spirit of the army, and consequently over the strength of the Government.

It will be considered, whether a measure, *not of concession*, but *of conciliation**, offered a prospect of greater evils

* These words have been, in the course of the discussion regarding the disturbances at Madras, as they were during their existence, greatly distorted

than a plan of division, such as Machiavelian politicians have sometimes employed against the public enemy ;—but which was now to be, for the first time, employed against the only safeguard of the state ;—a plan to make the King's troops look down on the Company's with the proud contempt of conquerors, and the Company's army feel towards the King's all the mortified pride and secret indignation natural to the vanquished ; a plan for suppressing a rebellion of European officers by clandestinely instigating a mutiny of native soldiers against them ; a plan for securing the Government by dividing and dispiriting the army, and for founding general tranquillity upon a monstrous balance of officers against soldiers, and of one army against another.

It will be ascribed to the unbending temper of Sir George Barlow, that he did not perceive the probability of amnesty being at length granted, after open resistance, by the humanity of the British Administration in India and England, almost as general as that of which, before the sword was drawn, he treated the proposal as every thing but a crime.

Future Governments will not be insensible to the dreadful dangers which have been incurred, even if the character of British officers should prevent the threatened evils from being realized ; and they will see, that though the policy

from their simple and plain meaning. *Concession*, I conceive, is to grant the original and substantial objects of the demands made by the mutinous army. To have restored the tent contract, to have promised an effort to obtain an equalization of their allowances with the officers of Bengal, would have been concessions : but if the exercise of a generous clemency, in pardoning those who had offended in a moment of general insanity, and to have held out hope to others of even deeper guilt, be deemed *concessions* which a Government *cannot make*, there can be no such thing as conciliation *in act:* and as to the profession of kindness and consideration, when the conduct observed by the ruling power is inflexible and severe in its measures, it can have no effect but that of aggravating men's feelings into greater crime.

of Great Britain has supported the cause of authority, yet her equitable benevolence has virtually disavowed these measures, by interposing to repair their harsher consequences.

POSTSCRIPT.

AFTER I had written these observations on the late disturbances at Madras, I perused a very able and ingenious article in the ninth number of the Quarterly Review, upon that subject. The first part of that article explains the progress of the violent proceedings of the Company's officers engaged in those disturbances, and enters into very full discussions to prove and establish the fact of their guilt. In almost all this part my sentiments differ little from those of the reviewer. I do not, however, agree with the opinions he has stated on the case of Lieutenant-Colonel Munro. He conceives, that if Government had allowed that officer to have been tried by a court martial, it would have been a base desertion, and a sacrifice of a public servant. I trust I have shown, that although Government had a *full legal right* to act as they did, a contrary conduct might have been adopted without any such desertion or sacrifice, and with every prospect of advantage to the public interests.

The reviewer dwells throughout the article upon the crude and violent Memorial to Lord Minto, and assumes, with great advantage to his argument, that it may be taken as a fair specimen of the sentiments of all the discontented officers at Madras. He is probably ignorant of the comparatively small number of those officers who approved of this intemperate production. He cannot, I think, be aware, that many of those whom he has blended in his general censure, merely because they were blended in the undistinguishing proscription of the Government of Fort St. George, never saw that document till it was published.

I have, in my observations on the disturbances at Madras, said little on the question of the suspension of Colonel Capper and Major Boles; but I conceive all that the reviewer has said upon that subject will be deemed by those who consider it attentively, as more ingenious than solid. The whole of that discussion would appear to resolve itself into a very short question. The act of disobedience to his superior, in a military officer or soldier, can alone be justified in a case where the civil law would punish his obedience. A great deal must of course be decided by the circumstances of the moment. "To your tents, O Israel!" would, in the present state of Great Britain, be an unobjectionable text. It certainly was not so in the reign of Charles the First. But we have only to suppose Major Boles on his trial before a civil court, for publishing, or aiding in the publication, of a seditious libel. Among the circumstances to be considered in such a case, that prompt and undeliberate obedience which it is the habit of an officer to give to the orders of his superiors, would assuredly be one of the most prominent; and an English jury would, I imagine, be slow in condemning an officer situated as Major Boles was. They would probably think, that the great and vital principle of prompt obedience, on which the existence of that armed force which guarded the civil community depended, was of too important and sacred a nature to have its plain meaning frittered away by casuists and lawyers. These reflections would certainly lead plain men to decide, that we ought not to refine too much upon such delicate points, and that no military order should be disobeyed, the illegality of which was not of so obvious a nature as to be clear to the most common understanding. But, after all, the justice or injustice of this act of authority is but a small part of a very large question. The wisdom and policy of the measure, (which is the point on which the character of the Government of Fort St. George is chiefly concerned,) appear, however, to be given up even by those who are the warm advocates of many other parts of that system which was pursued.

The writer of the review traces what he deems an exact similarity of character between Sir George Barlow's measures and those adopted by Lord Clive, in 1766, to quell a sedition among the officers of the Bengal army; and infers, from a general and sweeping conclusion, that the reputation of these two Governors must stand or fall by the same arguments. To those who are satisfied with the superficial and general facts,—that both Lord Clive and Sir George Barlow exercised power in India, that there were discontents and combinations among a part of the European officers of the native troops during their respective administrations, which terminated, on both occasions, in submission to authority,—the observations made in the Quarterly Review on this part of the subject will be satisfactory, and conclusive: but to such as examine the particulars of these two important events, and trace to its true cause the defection of the officers of the Bengal army in 1766, and then observe the open, military, and manly conduct of Lord Clive, there will appear much more grounds for a contrast than a comparison. The conduct of the officers of the Bengal army, their limited number, and the actual constitution of the native army* at that period of our dominion in India, make a still wider difference in all those considerations, that render the late measures of the Government of Madras, as they affect the personal attachment and fidelity of the sepoys to their European officers, dangerous to our future security. But supposing the difference in this respect did not exist, Lord Clive, when actually engaged in war, might have been compelled, by the conduct of officers, which the situation of affairs rendered doubly disgraceful, to adopt a measure that was most deeply injurious to those principles upon which our empire is founded. We have escaped this danger; but is that any reason for incurring a similar hazard? It has never been stated that the danger from weakening the respect and attachment of the sepoy for his officer was inevitable, and must be destructive to our power within a specific period. Its alarming tendency has been shown: and it is this which must be disproved, and the *absolute necessity* of having had resort to it established, before the course pursued

* The whole power was in the commanding officers of the sepoy battalion, and the native officers had much greater influenee than the European subalterns of the corps: *the latter were not even attached to companies.* It has been the labour of near twenty years to supersede the effects of this system, which was deemed bad, and to transfer the influence formerly enjoyed by the native officers to the European: and the eagerness with which the native officers grasped at a prospect of reviving their power, though it might have had a favourable operation for Government under that desperate expedient to which they had resort, must have given rise to dangerous feelings, and produced jealousy and distrust in that important link between the European and native officers, where complete confidence and cordiality is most essential to our safety.

in this instance by the Government of Fort St. George can be efficiently defended.

The reviewer appears resolved to deny every fact that can even palliate the guilt of the officers of the Madras army. He terms their desire to submit to Lord Minto a difference in point of form, "a saving to their pride, not to their consciences;" and he is amused with the assertion, that the love of their country had a decided operation in defeating their guilty proceedings. The man who reasons thus coolly upon such events, has probably never witnessed a scene at all resembling that of which he treats; or he would have discovered, that when passion seizes that ground which reason has abandoned, men act more under the influence of feelings than forms; and with minds deluded, but not debased, they make a vain attempt to reconcile the most opposite principles of conduct, and fall, *self-subdued,* by those virtues which are implanted too deeply in their hearts to be eradicated by the sudden action, however violent, of a guilty but transient impulse.

The able writer in the review conceives that he has at once discovered the chief cause of the late disturbances, and the best apology for the Company's officers concerned in them, in the constitution of the Company's service, and the habits of those that belong to it. The atmosphere they imbibe is calculated, in his opinion, to relax all just ideas of subordination ; and they are, he infers, predisposed, from such causes, to an opposition to the authority placed over them. Some disposition to resistance may no doubt be found in every community, civil as well as military, that ever existed ; and to the existence of this universal and natural feeling every excellence of human government may be traced. But let us suppose that this disposition had, from local circumstances and other causes, attained such a degree among the Company's officers in India, as to threaten the public tranquillity ; what does this prove ? It is, *if true to the extent stated in the review,* not an excuse for those who produced that crisis which has been described ; but an eulogium, and a very high one, upon the wisdom and vigour of those rulers of our Indian possessions, who have not only repressed this disposition to opposition, but have rendered those to whom it is ascribed the instruments of the advancement of the interests and glory of their country: and a reflecting man would probably find much more to admire, than condemn, even in that case* which is triumphantly brought forward to prove this assertion. When events led a wise and moderate Governor-General†, and an able and politic Indian minister‡, to prefer a course which certainly made many and important sacrifices of ordinary maxims of rule, but which led to a quiet and just settlement of all complaints; to the pursuit of a severe, inflexible system, which (anxious only for its own character) defends a principle at the hazard of a state: most persons, when they contemplated the great end, would at least pardon the means by which it was obtained, and perhaps see more of wisdom and generosity, than of "short-sightedness and "absurdity," in the measures of those who exercised their powers with such temper, forbearance, and indulgence, upon that memorable occasion. Those who endeavour to heap obloquy upon their names, in order to exalt a contrary course of proceeding, will find no support to their arguments from the conduct of the officers of the Bengal army subsequent to that occurrence: that has been exactly the reverse of what it ought to have been, agreeable to the conclusions of the writer of the review; and the great progress made in the discipline of that army, their strict adherence to every principle of order and subordination, (particularly on the occasion of the late agitations at Madras,) affords a most convincing proof of the wide difference between a spirit of discontent carried even to the extreme of opposition to authority, among a body of officers, (who, however lost to reason and duty for the moment, must soon return, instructed by their deviation, to that order on which their condition depends,) and a mutiny of common soldiers. Men solely educated in civil life are too apt to confound this great distinction: and to that ignorance of the different shades of military feeling which varies from the proud but rational submission of a cultivated mind, to the mere habit of mechanical obedience in one of a more vulgar mould, a great part of the evils which occurred at Madras may be ascribed.

* Disturbances in Bengal in 1794 and 1795.

† Lord Teignmouth. ‡ Lord Melville.

It has always been discovered, on a near view of human affairs, that smaller causes than the self-importance of man is willing to believe, produce the greatest changes in society. The difference between a general view of a subject, and a minute observation of all its parts, is immense: and to this difference, more than to any other cause, I am disposed to ascribe the opposite opinions I entertain, on many points of this large question, from the able writer of the review. He has, with a full sense of the advantage, dwelt upon those general principles that regulated the conduct of Sir George Barlow; and has enlarged, with great force and effect, upon their importance to good order and government. While he maintains this ground he is unassailable; and he seldom quits it: but if truth be the object of our search, we must go deeper. There perhaps never was an administration which exhibited, during the period of which we treat, so extraordinary a mixture of good principles, and a bad application of them; of an inflexible regard to form, and a total neglect of feeling, as that of the Governor of Fort St. George. It is from this reason, that every man of impartiality, who peruses a general statement of the late transactions at Madras, will give Sir George Barlow the highest praise: but if he looks further, and examines with a minute attention, not only his measures, but the season and mode of their execution; his admiration will infallibly diminish. He will be compelled (though perhaps reluctantly,) to abandon some abstract ideas regarding the beauty of general principles, which he may have long and fondly cherished, and to confess the force of that observation which experience taught Mr. Burke to make, upon all such general questions—"I have lost," said that great orator and statesman, "all confidence in your swaggering majors, having "always found that the truth lurked in the little minor of "*circumstances*."

In the conclusion of the article of the review the writer animadverts on the description given by Mr. Petrie of the cold and repulsive manners of Sir George Barlow; and in observing upon this "deficiency in the charm of demeanour," though he admits it must subtract from the influence of a statesman, he makes an allusive comparison (on the ground of common defects) between his character and that of some of the greatest names in history*, who, notwithstanding their defective manners, have, by the force of their superior genius, been able to command the support of mankind: and, to give more effect to this allusion, the reviewer quotes a public dispatch from Lord Minto, in which that nobleman ascribes the great unpopularity of Sir George Barlow to "a pure and inflexible discharge of ungrate-"ful, but sacred and indispensable duties." Self-defence has alone compelled me to discuss the acts of Sir George Barlow. On his character my opinion was long ago formed. It will be seen, that at the commencement of these disturbances I confidentially stated that opinion†. I then represented him as a man of excellent talent, of unsullied integrity, of indefatigable industry, and distinguished by long and meritorious services to the Company. I still retain that opinion; and no injustice of which he may be guilty towards me, shall ever prevent me from expressing it. I then foresaw that the defects of his character would, in his situation, probably produce very pernicious consequences. My opinion has been confirmed by the event. Experience seems to me to have most fully proved, that the very qualities which eminently fit a man for subordinate situations, may unfit him for the supreme; and that the rules which are necessary to the good order of many of the inferior departments, may, in their undistinguishing application, prove destructive in the general administration of a great state.

* William the Third, and Demosthenes.

† See the letters to Lord Wellesley and Sir A. Wellesley, p. 64, 65.

PART II.

A

NARRATIVE

OF THE

CONDUCT OF LIEUT.-COLONEL MALCOLM

DURING THE

DISTURBANCES IN THE MADRAS ARMY.

A NARRATIVE, &c.

When the first violent agitation appeared in the coast army I was at Bombay, in charge of a force destined for service in the Gulf of Persia. A part of this force was composed of Madras troops; and it became my peculiar care to prevent, as far as could be effected by the influence of reason and discipline, any contagion from spreading among those under my command. That I succeeded in this object is chiefly to be ascribed to the excellent character of the officers of this force, and to the distance at which they were from the scene of agitation. From what I heard before I left Bombay, on the 1st of May 1809, of the transactions on the coast, and the perfect knowledge I had of the character of the Governor of Fort St. George, I early apprehended the most unhappy result; and on the 18th of April 1809, I wrote to Lord Minto in the following terms:—

" We hear every day the most exaggerated reports " from Madras; but matters are, I fear, in a very bad " state. It is said a Memorial has been sent to your Lord- " ship for the removal of Sir George Barlow. I can " hardly credit this, though stated on very respectable " authority. I know that there is a personal irritation " against him, which exceeds all bounds; and this, how- " ever unjust and indefensible, will make it almost im- " possible for him to adjust matters by any means short " of coercion: and I trust in God such will not be found " necessary; for even success would not prevent the ruin-

"ous effects with which any measure of violence would "be attended. I cannot but think the great majority are "yet to be reclaimed to their duty; and I should think "one principal means of effecting this, would be your "Lordship's presence at Madras: and assuredly there "never was an occasion on which the active exertion of "all the great powers lodged in your Lordship's hands "was more necessary to the welfare of the state."

The impressions upon my mind at this moment will be still more forcibly shown by the following extract from a letter to the Marquis Wellesley, of the same date as that to Lord Minto, and upon the same subject:—

"Both Lord Minto and the Commander-in-Chief of "India should come to Madras; or, at all events, Lord "Minto. Whatever justice may be on the part of Sir "George Barlow, it will be ten times more difficult for "him to settle the question than any other; for the degree "of personal dislike which all ranks and classes have of "him, is not to be described. This may be, and I dare "say is, very indefensible: but it exists, and cannot be "changed; and the safety of the state should not be "thrown into hazard, if that hazard can be avoided by "the adoption of any measures that do not compromise "its dignity, or permanently weaken its authority. I am "quite satisfied of the purity and rectitude of Sir George "Barlow's character. The public never had a more "zealous or more laborious servant; he is devoted to his "duty, and has no enjoyment beyond that of performing "it; but his system is cold and inflexible, and proceeds "in its course without the slightest attention to the feel-"ings of those on whom it is to operate; and the present "distracted state of affairs at Madras is, I fear, a *comment*, "and *a melancholy one*, upon the result of *such systems*. "All the reforms which Sir George Barlow thought it his "duty to make, might have been made without giving rise "to any serious discontent, if he had proceeded with that "caution and that attention to the temper of the men

"which the situation in which he found the army required.
"They were in a state of great irritation when he arrived;
"and he was, from his reputation as a *reformer* and a
"*retrencher*, received with prejudices. The authority
"which should have controlled the army, acted a contrary
"part, and consequently made their ebullitions more to
"be dreaded. All these were subjects worthy of consi-
"deration; and relaxation from a severe system, till an
"insubordinate spirit was somewhat subdued, and the
"ruling authority fortified, would have not merely been
"warranted, but have been wise. At all events, the
"means of suppressing a disposition to violence should
"have been correctly calculated, before it was provoked
"to action. This, I fear, has not been the case; and it
"is most difficult to discover any means by which such a
"general spirit of discontent, as that which now exists,
"can be repressed. As it is unmixed with any thing like
"disaffection to the country, it will probably, if met with
"a firm and dignified spirit of conciliation, correct itself;
"and then every plan should be adopted that can prevent
"the recurrence of so dangerous an evil."

The following is the concluding paragraph of a long letter, dated the 16th of April 1809, which I wrote to Lord Wellington, on the same subject.

"I am yet very imperfectly informed of what has
"occurred. I shall soon know all. I proceed in a few
"days to Madras. *Had I been there at an earlier stage*
"*of this affair, I might have done good; but that expec-*
"*tation is over:* matters are too far gone; and there is
"too great irritation on the minds of all parties, to give
"hopes of reconciliation. You know Sir George Barlow:
"he is a highly respectable public servant. His prin-
"ciples of action are all right and correct; but his
"measures are often ill-timed, and consequently unfor-
"tunate. He generally leaves altogether out of the ques-
"tion, that which would engage the chief attention of an
"abler ruler,—*men's minds:* and though his cold system

"appears excellent in an abstract and general view, it
"often proves mischievous in its operation. He has
"another great fault, which looks so like an excellence at
"first glance, as to deceive most: he is perfectly in-
"flexible with regard to every thing that he deems a
"principle or rule. Now this is good on most occasions,
"but on some it is the height of folly; for, in the en-
"deavour to do a little good, are we justified in hazard-
"ing a world of mischief?"

Such were my sentiments, and such the view I took of the situation of affairs on the coast, before I left Bombay, from which I sailed on the 1st of May, and arrived at Madras on the 17th of that month. I was received by Sir George Barlow with even more than his usual kindness. He seemed to expect my personal efforts would aid greatly in allaying any little agitation that remained; for, at this moment, he was decidedly of opinion that the orders of the 1st of May had completely settled every thing that was serious, and that what appeared to remain, was merely the reaction of that seditious spirit which he had subdued. After a very few days' residence at Madras I became satisfied of the extent and danger of this error, and I laboured incessantly to convince Sir George Barlow that he was mistaken, and that a new, more extensive, and violent confederacy, than that which he had conquered, was in progress; the object of which was to obtain the repeal of the orders of the 1st of May. His unwillingness to believe this fact may be conceived, when I state, that he would not admit the conduct of the subsidiary force at Hyderabad, who, in a public address, disclaimed the compliment he had paid their fidelity, to be evidence of its truth.

I was not discouraged by that strong disinclination which I observed in Sir George Barlow to credit every information I gave him upon this subject, but continued to press upon him the urgency of the case, and to entreat him to adopt measures calculated to remedy so desperate and general an evil, before it had attained that maturity to which it was fast approaching. The great and generous object was, I said, to save, not to destroy, a body of brave and meritorious, though infatuated men, who were rushing upon their own ruin. They had (I not once, but a hundred times repeated to Sir George Barlow,) a more serious quarrel than that with Government, they had quarrelled with themselves; and, unless he could adopt some measure that would restore them to their own good opinion, every attempt to establish order and subordination would be vain, as they were goaded on to further guilt by a torturing sense of that into which they had already plunged. On being, at one of these conferences, desired by Sir George Barlow to suggest what I thought would promote this end, I proposed (if the expedient had his approbation,) to draw up an address to him from the Company's officers on direct opposite principles to those seditious papers that I knew were then in circulation; and to give, by this measure, a shape to that feeling which still existed in the army, but which was scattered, and, from having no union, was repressed by the combined action of the discontented and turbulent. This address was as follows:

"We, the undersigned officers of the Madras establish-"ment, trust that the very extraordinary and unprece-"dented situation in which we are placed by some recent "occurrences, will plead our excuse for an address which "has no object but that of vindicating ourselves, as a "body, from those serious imputations to which we con-"ceive it possible we may become liable, from the nature "of late proceedings in the army to which we belong; and "to assert our devoted allegiance to our King, our un-"alterable attachment to our Country, and our consequent "respect and submission to the laws and acts of that local "Government under which we are placed, and whose "commands it is our duty, under all circumstances, to "obey, as those of a legitimate branch of the constitution "of our country.

"It would be painful to retrace all those events which

" have led to the present unhappy state of feeling in the " army, and have compelled Government to those measures " which it has judged proper to adopt: we shall therefore " content ourselves with expressing our conviction, that, " however far they might have been carried by the warmth " of the moment, none of our brother officers who were " concerned in those proceedings which have been deemed " so reprehensible by Government, ever harboured an " idea in their minds that was irreconcileable to their " allegiance as subjects, or their duty as soldiers. Go- " vernment must be fully acquainted with the rise and " progress of all the proceedings to which we allude, and " can refer to its true cause any apparent excess, either " in expression or act, that may have marked the conduct " of any individuals: and it will, we are assured, separate " actions which have their motive in generous and honour- " able though mistaken feeling, from any deliberate design " of showing a spirit of contumely and insubordination to " that authority which it is their duty to obey, and whose " orders they could never dispute, without a total sacrifice " of their characters as good soldiers and loyal subjects: " and we feel perfectly satisfied there is not one officer in " this army who would not sooner lose his life than forfeit " his claim to such cherished distinctions.

" We cannot have a doubt but it must have been " with extreme reluctance that Government has adopted " the measures it has done, against those of our brother " officers who have more particularly incurred its dis- " pleasure, from the forward share they took, or were " supposed to take, in the proceedings which have met " with its disapprobation: and though we never can pre- " sume to question in any shape the acts of that Govern- " ment which it is our duty to obey, it is impossible for " us to contemplate the present situation of those officers " without sentiments of the deepest concern: and when " we reflect on the general high reputation, and the well- " merited distinction, which some of them have, by their "valour and ability, obtained in the public service, we "should be unjust to the characters of our superiors both "in India and England, if we did not entertain a hope "that their case would meet with a favourable and in- "dulgent consideration. But we feel restrained from "dwelling upon this subject, as we are aware its very "mention might be deemed improper in an address, the "great and sole object of which is to correct misappre- "hension, and to convey a solemn assurance of our con- "tinued and unalterable adherence to the same principles "of loyalty and attachment to our King and Country, and "of respect and obedience to the Government we serve, "that have ever distinguished the army to which we be- "long."

The object of this address was to reconcile men to themselves; and it therefore ceded as much as was possible in its expression to the predominant feelings of the moment; but its principle was not to be mistaken: and the unqualified and decided declaration which it contained, of attachment and of implicit obedience to Government, must have had the certain effect of separating all those by whom this address was subscribed, from persons who cherished contrary sentiments. But the great object of this measure was to concentrate and embody the good feelings of the army; to hoist a standard to which men could repair, whose minds revolted at the proceedings then in progress, but who were deterred by shame, fear of reproach, and want of union, from expressing an open difference of opinion from the more violent. I was assured at the moment that I suggested this measure, of its partial success, and not without some hopes that it would be general; but I perfectly knew, that if the senior and more reflecting part of the officers of the army signed an address that pledged them to an active discharge of their duty to Government, all danger of the remainder having recourse to desperate extremes, was at an end; for the influence of the senior part of the army over the native troops was decided; and this open declaration would at once have drawn a line of separation betwixt the moderate and reasonable, and the turbulent, which would have deprived the leaders of the latter of their chief source of strength, which obviously lay in their being able to deceive the multitude they guided, by persuading them that the cause was general*, and that many, whom prudence made reserved, would join them the moment they ventured on a bolder line of action.

In my anxiety to reconcile his mind to the adoption of this measure, I more than once modified the expression of the address; and softened, and in some instances struck out, those passages which he seemed to think were most objectionable I also took every pains to satisfy his mind that it should never be known he had been consulted on the subject. It was my intention to endeavour to obtain the high and honoured name of Colonel Close at the head of this address; and after adding those of several other officers of rank and estimation, whose sentiments I knew would be favourable to such an object, to circulate it with an appeal to the good sense of the whole army. Sir George Barlow certainly hesitated regarding this measure, for he kept the draft of the address two or three days, and then returned it with a rejection of the expedient, grounded on his dislike to the adoption of any step that was contrary to the established rules of his Government; to his fear, that receiving such an address in a favourable manner might in some degree sacrifice † his dignity, and, by doing so, weaken that authority to which he trusted for the settlement of that partial spirit of discontent which still existed. It was in vain that I argued that the common rules of Government were adapted for common times, and that in

These were the persons who fabricated those reports that were circulated and believed by numbers, respecting promises of aid and support from the officers of Bengal and Bombay.

† *This fear of being thought afraid*, is, perhaps, of all motives of human action one of the weakest, though it wears a mask of boldness, and under that is often productive of infinite mischief.

emergencies like the present, which presented nothing but difficulties, those should be chosen which were likeliest to effect the object at the least hazard to the state. All my reasoning was ineffectual; and I was most reluctantly compelled to abandon this project, from which I at that moment expected great success. Every future event has satisfied my mind I was not too sanguine. I conscientiously believe, if it had been adopted, though numbers might, by their obstinacy and violence, have merited and received punishment, yet the large body of Company's officers on the Madras establishment would have restored the character of the army to which they belonged. The extremes which have occurred, with all their baneful, and perhaps irremediable consequences, would have been avoided; and assuredly the prospect even of attaining such ends and of averting such evils, was worth a slight departure from a common rule, and might have justified some small deviation from the rigid system pursued by the Government of Madras.

To show in the most convincing light the correct view I took at that moment of the actual state of affairs, and the very opposite sentiments entertained by Sir George Barlow, I shall here quote some passages from the private letters that I wrote from the 3d to the 15th of June, (which includes the whole of the period of which I am now speaking,) to Lord Minto and his private secretary. The following is a copy of my letter to Lord Minto of the 3d of June.

" I have delayed from day to day writing to your Lord-
" ship, till I could inform myself of the real state of affairs
" at this distracted Presidency; and I wish I could, in
" discharging my duty towards you, confirm those im-
" pressions which *I believe you have received*, of the
" general good effect produced by the orders of the 1st
" of May, and of the return of the officers of this Presi-
" dency to the principles of good order and subordination.
" The very contrary I believe to be the fact: and I am

" satisfied that general spirit of discontent which has long
" pervaded this army, had never more danger in it than
" at this moment. I differ with Sir George Barlow (who
" has behaved with the most flattering kindness to me, and
" given me his complete* confidence,) upon this point;
" but I have too good a reason to rely upon my sources
" of information. Besides, Can there be a greater indi-
" cation of this spirit than has been exhibited in the con-
" duct of the subsidiary force at Hyderabad? They have,
" in an address to the whole army, disclaimed all title to
" the thanks bestowed upon them, and publicly avowed,
" that they not only shared the sentiments of the army,
" as expressed in their former addresses, but felt deeply
" for their brother officers, who had been arbitrarily sus-
" pended for just and honourable actions, and were deter-
" mined to contribute to their support in a firm, legal, and
" moderate manner. These are, as nearly as my memory
" serves, the words of this address: but a copy has pro-
" bably been sent to your Lordship; as one has, I under-
" stand, been received at head-quarters. Nothing can
" exceed the present irritation: and it has, I am assured,
" gone much greater lengths than Sir George Barlow can
" bring himself to believe. I confess I am not without
" some apprehension of misfortune: and however reluc-
" tant my mind is to believe that men can ever be so des-
" perate as to forget their duty to their country, I cannot
" resist evidence; and I certainly have seen what con-
" vinces me that the most dangerous combinations are
" formed, and conducted on principles entirely hostile to
" order and good government. I have most frequent,
" and indeed daily, communications with Sir George
" Barlow upon this subject; and have not only given him
" every information I possess, but every opinion I have
" formed; and have the highest reason to be satisfied with

* I thought so at that period, though I have been since convinced I was mistaken.

"the manner in which my communications are received. "He is as satisfied as I am, that the best reliance which "Government has at this moment, is the remaining good "feeling of the army itself. We differ a little as to the "best means of bringing this into action. He is adverse "to every expedient that is *not in consistence with usage*. "I think that those means are best which will most speedily "effect the object in a manner that will be satisfactory to "the pride and loyal feelings of the great majority of the "army, and yet not compromise in the slightest degree "the dignity of Government. The irritation that has "been caused and kept up by those acts, which Govern-"ment has taken from private information or reports of "speeches at table, &c. is not to be conceived. The "most extreme emergency can only justify any public "authority opening such dangerous and suspicious chan-"nels, and they should be closed the moment the danger "is past. At present I am satisfied, (and so is Sir George "Barlow,) it is better to incur any hazard than have fur-"ther resort to such unpopular and uncertain means of "detecting delinquency: and he is resolved to let military "law have its free course, in the conviction, that his best "chance of reclaiming a body of honourable though mis-"guided men, to their duty, is by showing he has not lost "confidence in them.

"Sir George Barlow has hopes this agitation will sub-"side* of itself. I cannot think so. They are maddened "with a thousand reflections, and with none more than "the shame and ruin which their rash proceedings have "brought on some of the most popular of their brother "officers. They have, in fact, not only quarrelled with "Government, but with themselves; and such quarrels

* Sir George Barlow not only thought so, but must, from the Governor General's letter to the secret committee of the 12th of October 1809, have conveyed the same impression to Lord Minto. The merit of foresight will not assuredly be claimed as one among the talents that were displayed by the Governor of Fort St. George upon this memorable occasion.

" are difficult to settle. Besides, they are secretly goaded
" on by a thousand discontented men, who, defeated in
" other objects, wish to throw this Government into con-
" fusion ?

On the 12th of June I again wrote to his lordship:

" I wish I could say affairs here were in a better state;
" but I cannot yet agree with Sir George Barlow that the
" discontent is subsiding Addresses have come from
" every part of the army to the principal officers sus-
" pended by the orders of the 1st of May, containing
" assurances of support, &c. These, fortunately, have
" not yet been brought under the eye of Government. I
" say fortunately; because it would be impossible for Go-
" vernment, in consistence with its past proceedings, to
" pass such addresses unnoticed; and I should regret to
" see it obliged to notice them at a moment when the good
" sense and good feeling of the army seems lost, and the
" whole appears under the influence of blind passion. Sir
" George Barlow has put an end to all proceedings grounded
" on private information, and has resolved to maintain that
" dignified line which never stoops to suspicion, and makes
" men worthy of confidence by boldly giving it to them.
" *If this is persevered in*, it will do great good; for it will
" excite into action the remaining good feeling of the
" army, which, though dormant, must be considerable;
" and which forms, at this moment, the great, if not the
" only, strength of Government."

And upon the 15th of June I wrote to his Lordship's son and private secretary, Mr. John Elliott, as follows:

" With regard to this army I have already written to
" Lord Minto. I am satisfied he has never had a full idea
" of the danger to which the public interests are exposed,
" or I think he would have come to this spot. I am far
" from meaning to state that Sir George Barlow has not
" communicated all he knew or thought: but, in the first
" place, I am satisfied he has been, generally speaking,
" badly informed; and, in the next, he has been endea-

" vouring to persuade himself that there was no danger, " and even now he tries to think every thing will subside; " though he knows (*for I have told him*) that papers of " the most objectionable nature are in circulation, and that " the most violent measures have been, and are, contem- " plated. It is impossible to convey to men who are calm " and think rationally, any idea of the state of this army " All the respectable men in it appear to suffer a set of " mad-headed boys to take the lead: and the greatest " merit I see any man claim, is that of being passive; " though all confess it is a period at which one step will " involve the country in all the horrors of a civil war: " and there are numbers (such is the insanity that has got " head,) that desire to accelerate that event.

" You may be satisfied I would not even hint at a state " of affairs so shocking to contemplate, if I had not the " strongest grounds for what I state: but I have seen the " greater part of their correspondence, *and know, and have* " *informed Sir George Barlow*, of the extent to which " matters have proceeded, and of the increase of irritation " that has been lately produced: particularly by that ill- " judged and unmerited compliment to the force at Hy- " derabad, who, from being moderate, have, with the " customary zeal of converts, become the most violent; " and would (but for the timely exercise of Colonel Mon- " tresor's personal influence,) have forced a paper a few " days ago upon Government, which it must have noticed " most seriously; and that notice was expected by some " of the maddest to be the signal of some very violent mea- " sures. This remonstrance, as I said before, has been " stopt; but there is, I fear, too much reason to conclude " others of the same character will be forwarded. I know " not whether Lord Minto is informed of all these circum- " stances; but it is proper he should know them, as they " refer to one of the most serious dangers that can assail " the Empire under his charge. I enjoy Sir George Bar- " low's fullest confidence upon this subject; but he has,

"I believe, *more congenial counsellors*, who are fonder of "maintaining the consistency of Government upon paper, "than of tranquillizing the minds of a meritorious and "honourable, though misguided body of men: but as-"suredly every means should be adopted which human "wisdom can suggest, to reclaim them to temper and at-"tachment, provided always such means do not compro-"mise the strength and dignity of Government. Conces-"sions cannot be made to demand; but men may, perhaps, "by management, be reconciled to themselves and the "state by something short of concession. Sir George "Barlow has rather an exaggerated opinion of my per-"sonal influence; and he thinks, I believe, it will effect "what I only expect from the united good feeling of the "army. I have, however, done all I can; and shall con-"tinue, under all circumstances, my most ardent efforts in "the cause of good order and government."

I heard, towards the end of June, of some extraordinary proceedings that had taken place regarding the European regiment stationed at Masulipatam, in consequence of a dispute between the Lieutenant-Colonel commanding and the officers of the corps. The substance of these proceedings* may be given in a few words. Lieutenant-Colonel Innes, the day after he joined the regiment (the 7th of May), dined at the mess, where a toast was given, "The "friends of the army;" to which he objected, and proposed it to be changed for one of less equivocal meaning—"The Madras army." This was not assented to, and he left the table. Next day he wrote an account of this circumstance to head-quarters, but *desired it should not be noticed*, as he expected an apology from those officers whose conduct he considered as most disrespectful. The moment his letter reached Madras, an order was transmitted, directing Lieutenant David Forbes, who was said to

* See Lieutenant-Colonel Malcolm's letter to General Gowdie, in the Appendix.

be the person who had given the toast, to proceed, at a few hours' warning, to the Fort of Condapilly, a solitary and far from healthy post, at the distance of forty miles, and one at which there was not *one* man of the corps to which he belonged. Lieutenant Maitland, who was reported to have seconded the toast, was, by the same order, deprived of his station of Quarter-Master. These measures, combined with an imprudent declaration of Colonel Innes, that the corps would be disbanded if a young officer refused to accept the vacant station of Quarter-Master, (by which probably it was only meant that that event might be apprehended, if such a spirit of insubordination continued,) threw the officers of the regiment into a great ferment, and led to their making a representation to head-quarters, earnestly soliciting the benefit of regular military trial, and deprecating the disgrace to which they were exposed from such punishments being inflicted, without the slightest opportunity being given to individuals of vindicating themselves from the private accusations made against them.

I was quite satisfied, from what I heard of those proceedings, of which I have only given the outline, that they were more than severe; and were calculated, in even ordinary times, to produce much irritation; and I therefore was not at all surprised at their aggravated effect at a period of such general agitation. Soon after these events had occurred, I was informed by Admiral Drury, that he had, in consequence of an order from the Duke of York, desiring all the men of his Majesty's regiments employed as marines to be landed, applied to the Government of Fort St. George for some men; and that a detachment had been ordered from the regiment at Masulipatam, for which a frigate and sloop of war were to sail that evening. Many circumstances had made me, about this period, very reluctant to press the attention of Sir George Barlow to a danger, the existence of which he *appeared resolved* not to believe; but I could not help, upon this occasion, stating to his private secretary, Lieutenant-Colonel Barclay, all I thought upon the subject. The following is an extract of my note to that confidential officer.

"The great object at present, is not to agitate, in any "way, (if it can be avoided,) any of those questions which "have disturbed the temper of the army; and to restore "that, by every means short of concession, to its proper "tone. To effect this, we must trust in large points to "the action of the good feeling of the army itself, and "small questions will soon die of neglect. Now it occurs "to me, the ordering a large detachment of the European "regiment at this moment on board his Majesty's ships, is "liable to much misrepresentation, and is calculated to "increase discontent. This has not been usual; and, "after the conduct of the officers of the regiment, it will "be considered as a punishment: and if it is so, it will, "from its nature, have no good effect; for it will be refer-"red to a desire to divide a corps, which men will say "never could have arisen, if Government had been con-"fident in their obedience and attachment. The corps "itself will receive this order as an additional stigma on "their character; and, in the heated state they are in, I "should not be surprised if they went to greater extremi-"ties than they already have gone; and, if the accounts "I have heard of their proceedings are correct, they "have been bolder in their expressions of discontent than "any corps in the service. All this is perhaps very "improbable; but still no man acquainted with the pre-"sent state of affairs can say it is impossible; and why "incur the most distant hazard of aggravating men's "feelings by a measure of such trifling consequence? "No man could, at this moment, have recommended, as "a political measure, such a wretched expedient as that "of dividing this corps in the manner proposed; and if "it is merely to comply with a requisition of the Admiral "for marines, he might take them, as has been the usage, "from any one of the King's regiments, or might go "without, rather than give cause to misrepresentation at "such a moment. If all or any of the officers of the "European regiment merit punishment, let them be "punished in an open manner, agreeable to usage, and "my life upon the consequence: but to think of sending "one here, and one there*, is only to show weakness, and "to give grounds to the wicked to circulate aggravated "reports, and to kindle the flame of discord and discon-"tent. Pardon this hasty note, and tear it†. You will "understand what I mean perfectly. *Depend upon it,* "*it is trifles of this nature which merit all the attention of* "*Government at this moment.*"

I did not receive any answer from Lieutenant-Colonel Barclay till next morning; when, after stating the hurry that prevented him from writing, and the causes which had made Government order this detachment, he states his belief, grounded on his knowledge of Masulipatam as a station, that there will be a competition between both officers and men to proceed as marines; and concludes by saying, "I shall only add further, that there is no guard-"ing against wilful misrepresentations, and that those "who are obliged to act, must, in such cases as the pre-"sent, be satisfied with the uprightness of their inten-"tions."

Every thing that I had foreseen occurred. The arrival of the orders for the marines occasioned an instant mutiny of the garrison of Masulipatam, and precipitated that crisis which it was of such great consequence to avoid. Sir George Barlow felt this occurrence as a serious evil; and, in a long conversation I had with him upon the

* Lieutenant Maitland, the dismissed quarter-master, was ordered to command the marines; and Lieutenant Forbes, who had been banished to Condapilly, was directed to proceed to relieve an officer of the regiment on duty at Prince of Wales's Island. This second punishment was a torturing revival of those wrongs, of which not only the parties, but all the officers of the corps, had before, with some justice, complained.

† Lieutenant-Colonel Barclay afterwards returned me the original note.

subject, he expressed the extremest anxiety to prevent those bad consequences which were to be expected to result, by the adoption of every moderate and conciliatory means that he could use, without a compromise of the authority and dignity of Government. He told me he had rejected all the violent measures that had been proposed, of coercing the garrison into submission by the employment of his Majesty's troops; as such, he was convinced, would cause a general rupture, which he still hoped would be avoided; and which, at all events, it was most important to retard. His anxiety on this occasion was much increased by the receipt, at the same period, of a highly improper address from the officers of the subsidiary force at Hyderabad; and he desired my opinion on the best course to be pursued on so alarming an emergency. I advised a line that appeared to me likely to arrest the progress of men standing on a precipice of guilt. Every hour gained gave time for the operation of reason; and if that should fail, it was still of consequence that Government should be more prepared than it was at that moment for the occurrence of a rupture with its army. On these grounds, I recommended that an officer of rank should be sent to Masulipatam to assume the command, and that he should be appointed president of a committee to inquire into the causes of the mutiny, and report their proceedings to Government, *who would, when the information upon this subject was complete, adopt measures for the prosecution and punishment of the most guilty.* In this proceeding there was an appearance of great temper and moderation; no serious sacrifice of dignity was made; and time (which, for reasons before stated, appeared the great object,) was gained: and all those effects which must have attended the detachment of a force against the garrison, or the equally unwise proceeding of attempting (before either reason had time to operate, or the means of coercion were prepared) to arrest or confine any individual, were avoided. On Sir George Barlow's expressing his assent to my suggestions, I offered, in the warmth of my zeal, to proceed to Masulipatam. He accepted this offer with great apparent pleasure; and he evidently thought that the appointment of an officer who was known to enjoy his confidence, and who had so publicly professed a conciliatory disposition, proclaimed the character of the act: and the nomination of Lieutenant-Colonel William Berkley and Major Evans to aid me, (two officers who are now no more, but who, while they lived, enjoyed in an eminent degree the love and respect of all ranks in the army to which they belonged,) was a full confirmation (if any had been wanted) of the nature of this measure*. If it had been possible for me to have mistaken Sir George Barlow in the conversation I had with him on the morning he received this intelligence, I was completely confirmed by what passed in the evening after I had been in the fort, and, in the office of the commander of the forces, (General Gowdie,) had a discussion with some of the officers of the general staff upon the whole of this subject. One of those officers, who was known to enjoy the chief share of Sir George Barlow's confidence, stated at this conference, that movements of corps would be immediately ordered that would place the native troops under the com-

* The following paragraph of a letter from Lieutenant-Colonel Montresor to Lieutenant-Colonel Doveton, dated Secundrabad, the 10th July, 1809, is a proof of the light in which this measure was viewed, and the use made of it to reclaim the most violent to duty and submission.—"When the "address was forwarded from Jaulnah, the officers could not have known "that the Government of Madras had taken such steps as were most "likely to quiet the public mind, in consequence of the unpleasant state "of affairs at Masulipatam. Lieutenant-Colonel Malcolm, whose sound "sense, knowledge of the army, and conciliatory manners, peculiarly "qualified him for the difficult task of allaying the ferment in the northern "division of the army, has already arrived at Masulipatam, and a com-"mittee has been ordered to inquire into the late occurrences, composed "of three officers among the most popular in the army: therefore I am "sure the officers of Jaulnah will see the bad effects of forwarding an "address, at this moment, of any nature whatever, as it could only tend "to add to the irritation of the public mind." Vide printed Correspondence, No. 2, page 35.

plete check of his Majesty's regiments; and that the Governor should, in his opinion, have no hesitation in throwing himself at once upon the King's army. I could not but treat such sentiments with some warmth, as being altogether incompatible with that ardent wish which was professed of reclaiming the Company's officers to their duty. The very knowledge, I observed to General Gowdie, of such sentiments being held and declared, was in itself sufficient to drive men to extremes. The General fully acquiesced in my opinion. Another officer of the staff, who was also a principal adviser of the Governor, said upon this occasion, that he understood I was a friend to concessions that would degrade the Government; that his advice had been, to send a detachment to attack Masulipatam; and that unless I could, the moment I went there, send Major Storey and the other ringleaders under a guard to Madras, evil, instead of good, must result from my mission. I repelled this gentleman's attack with a warmth that produced interference to prevent a personal dispute, and concluded by telling him, that I was now aware of the true character of those sentiments entertained by the persons who had the chief influence over Sir George Barlow's mind; and that, with that knowledge, I should certainly not proceed to Masulipatam, as I saw the probability of measures being adopted, in my absence, of a directly opposite character to those I was desired to execute; and the only consequence I should anticipate, was failure and loss of character. Some explanations were made, but none that dispelled the alarm I had taken at the sentiments which I had just heard. I went immediately to the Governor, to whom I mentioned all that had passed: and I can most solemnly affirm, that Sir George Barlow gave me, at this second conference, every assurance that could be given to satisfy my mind. He declared he would not listen to any such violent counsels* as I had heard;

* Two days after I went away, and when no event had occurred of any consequence, he was persuaded (as has been before shown) to commence

that he gave me his entire confidence, and vested me with the fullest discretion to act in all respects as I thought proper, in my endeavours to reclaim the deluded men, to whom I was proceeding, to reflection and duty; and that he was satisfied the honour of his Government was perfectly safe in my hands. Not one word was mentioned, at this conference, regarding my commencing my proceeding by an appeal to the men, or by confining those officers who had been most active in the mutiny. It was, indeed, evident that the first of these acts would have caused a desperation in the minds of the officers, that must have led to that instant rupture which *it was the object of my mission to avoid*; and, with regard to the second, a military court of inquiry had been ordered to investigate the whole of the proceedings at Masulipatam, chiefly, if not exclusively, with the view of enabling Government to gain time, without loss of reputation; and any precipitate proceedings against the ringleaders would have been an obvious sacrifice of that great object.

Such were the sentiments of Sir George Barlow at the moment I was deputed to Masulipatam: at least such were the impressions which all his observations made upon my mind. He determined at this moment to return the address from Hyderabad, and to write a letter to the commanding officer of that force in terms calculated to show his forbearance, and indeed to evince to the violent and misguided officers of that station the same spirit of temperate and conciliatory disposition as had led him to depute me to Masulipatam. He desired me to make a memorandum of what I conceived he should write upon this occasion. I instantly drew out the following.

"Substance of a letter to the commanding officers at "Hyderabad and Jaulnah.

the plan for placing the native corps under check of his Majesty's regiments, and the orders were sent to Hyderabad for the march of the 2d of the 10th to Goa.

"Expressing the great regret and disapprobation with "which Government has receivec a Memorial from the "officers of the subsidiary force, soliciting it to rescind "the orders of the 1st of May.

"Pointing out in a calm but forcible manner the "dangerous tendency of such addresses, and the total im-"possibility of complying with such a request; stating that "Government is only fulfilling a sacred duty when it ex-"horts the officers who have signed and forwarded these "papers to reflect most seriously upon the consequences "which a perseverance in such measures must produce. "It owes this warning and exhortation to a body of men, "who, acting under warm and erroneous impressions, "have for a moment forgot what is due to their own high "character, and to that Government under which they "are placed. The motives of this expostulation with the "officers of the subsidiary force will not be misunder-"stood; but it is necessary that they should distinctly "know, that while Government can and does make every "allowance for that momentary delusion and irritation "which a variety of circumstances have been calculated "to produce, that it will never either abandon or com-"promise its authority; and that it will, if compelled to "act, maintain, under every extreme and at every hazard, "those principles of obedience and subordination, with-"out which, it is satisfied, neither it nor the army can "exist."

With this memorandum Sir George Barlow was perfectly pleased, and desired me to give it the form of a letter, and deliver it to Lieutenant-Colonel Barclay, that it might be dispatched next day*. I did so, and carried the copy of the memorandum with me to Masulipatam,

* Instead of sending this letter, the order for the march of a battalion from Hyderabad to Goa, in prosecution of the plan for dividing the sepoy corps, was sent two days after my departure, and provoked (as was, under such circumstances, to have been expected) open resistance and rebellion.

for which place I sailed on the 2d of July 1809, the whole of the circumstances to which I have alluded having taken place on the day preceding.

I landed at Masulipatam on the 4th of July; and the journal of my proceedings at that place, with the extracts of my letters to Sir George Barlow, General Gowdie, and Lieutenant-Colonel Barclay, and of the letters I received from the latter officer (all of which form numbers of the Appendix), will give the clearest and most faithful account of the manner in which I executed the arduous task that an imprudent, but I hope not an illaudable, zeal led me to undertake. During my residence at that place I continued active in my endeavours to disseminate, by letters to different quarters of the army, such sentiments as I thought calculated to counteract the poison of those inflammatory papers that were then in circulation: and the extract from my letter addressed to a respectable field officer (Lieutenant-Colonel McLeod), under date the 20th of July 1809, which forms a number of the Appendix, will show the complete and just view I took at that period of the result of the violent proceedings of the army.

I left Masulipatam on the night of the 22d of July, and arrived at Madras on the morning of the 26th, having travelled two hundred and ninety miles in little more than three days. I knew of the flagrant act of disobedience which the subsidiary force at Hyderabad had committed, in refusing to allow the 2d battalion of the 10th regiment to march to Goa, to which station it had been ordered in prosecution of the plan for dividing the native corps so as to place them under the check of his Majesty's regiments *. I thought it probable that this event would give

* This irritating and imprudent order (which has been before noticed) was sent to Hyderabad a day or two after I sailed; and the same influence that obtained the adoption of this measure, prevented the dispatch of the letter to the commanding officers of Hyderabad and Jaulnah, which I drafted, and which Sir George Barlow at the moment approved, and *assured me he would send.*

rise to some strong measures on the part of Government, and I was most anxious to communicate all the information I had collected before any such were adopted: but, though no danger could have resulted from delay, the Governor, who knew I would be at Madras on the morning of the 26th, did not deem it necessary to wait even for a few hours, though strongly urged to do so by Major-General Gowdie , the commander of the forces; and the moment of my arrival was that of the execution of the orders of the 26th of July for the separation of the officers from their men. I did not see Sir George Barlow till next day: and the cold manner in which I was received, the slighting view which I saw was taken of my efforts at Masulipatam, and the reserve maintained, not only by him, but by others, left me without a doubt that I was no longer honoured with his confidence; which I was now, indeed, convinced I had never possessed but in a very limited degree. I therefore resolved, in future, to confine myself to an obedience of any orders I might receive, and no longer to expose myself to that failure and disgrace which must always attend the person who acts as a confidential agent, on delicate and important occasions, to one with whose proceedings his mind does not accord, whose confidence he does not enjoy, and of whose plans he is but imperfectly informed. But, before I proceed to explain the subsequent part I took in these transactions, it will be proper to offer some remarks on the observations made in the letter, under date 10th September, 1809, from the Government of Fort St. George to the Secret Committee of the Court of Directors, re pecting my conduct at Masulipatam. The following is an extract from the letter from the Governor of Fort St. George upon this subject.

" On receiving intelligence of the mutiny, we appointed " Lieutenant-Colonel Malcolm, in whose zeal and talents " we entertained the fullest confidence, to the command

The Major-General assured me of this fact.

" of the Madras European regiment, and the garrison of " Masulipatam, for the purpose of re-establishing the " authority of Government over the troops, inquiring into " the causes of the mutiny, and placing the most guilty of " the offenders under arrest. Lieutenant-Colonel Malcolm " was not furnished with any written instructions: it was " left to his discretion to adopt such measures as circum-" stances might render advisable, with the view to the " accomplishment of the objects of his deputation.

" Lieutenant-Colonel Malcolm immediately proceeded " by sea to Masulipatam. On his arrival he found that " the officers of the garrison had formed themselves into " a committee, in which every officer had a voice. The " greatest anarchy and confusion prevailed; and it was " with difficulty that he prevailed on the officers to " acknowledge his authority.

" As it never was in the contemplation of the Govern-" ment to disband the European regiment, it was expected " that Lieutenant-Colonel Malcolm would have taken the " earliest opportunity to communicate to the men a distinct " and public disavowal of that intention on the part of the " Government, and have employed the most strenuous " exertions to recall the men to a sense of their duty, by " impressing upon their minds the degree of guilt and " danger in which their officers, for purposes entirely per-" sonal to themselves, had endeavoured to involve them. " It was also expected that Lieutenant-Colonel Malcolm, " by establishing his influence and authority over the " troops composing the garrison, would have secured " their obedience, and by that measure have deprived " the officers of the power of prosecuting their designs, " and brought the leaders to trial for their mutinous con-" duct.

" Lieutenant-Colonel Malcolm appears, however, to " have adopted a course of proceedings entirely different " from that which we had in view in deputing him to " Masulipatam. He abstained from making any direct

" communication to the men: and when we authorized " him, with the view of detaching the troops from the " cause of their officers, to proclaim a pardon to the " European and native soldiers for the part which they " might have taken in the mutiny, he judged it proper to " withhold the promulgation of the pardon, from an ap- " prehension (as stated in his letter to our President, dated " the 18th of July) of irritating the minds of the European " officers, and driving them to despair.

" To this apparent unreasonable forbearance and atten- " tion to the feelings of the officers, who had, by their " acts of violence and aggression, forfeited all claims to " such consideration, may, we conceive, be ascribed " Lieutenant-Colonel Malcolm's failure in the establish- " ment of any efficient control over the garrison: and he " appears to have been principally occupied, during the " period of his residence at Masulipatam, in negociations " with the disorderly committees;, calculated, in our " opinion, to compromise rather than establish his au- " thority; and in fruitless attempts to induce them, by " argument, to return to their duty, and abandon the " criminal combination in which they had engaged. " Lieutenant-Colonel Malcolm's reasons for pursuing this " line of conduct, and for recommending to us the " adoption of conciliatory and temporizing measures, are " detailed in his letters to our President, dated the 4th, " 5th, and 6th of July. In those letters he states, that " the officers at Masulipatam had received assurances " from most of the military stations of the army, applaud- " ing their conduct, and promising them effectual sup- " port; that the whole army were united in a resolution to " oppose the authority of Government; that there was " not a single corps, from Ganjam to Cape Comorin, which " was not prepared to break out into open rebellion. The " measures recommended by Lieutenant-Colonel Malcolm, " as constituting, in his opinion, the only means of avert- " ing the most dreadful calamities, consisted of a modified "repeal of the orders of the 1st of May; the restoration "to the service, and to their appointments, of all the "officers whom we had found it necessary to suspend or "remove; with an intimation to the army, that their "claims to Bengal allowances would be brought to the "notice of the Honourable the Court of Directors. Lieu-"tenant-Colonel Malcolm returned to Madras, on the "arrival of Major-General Pater at Masulipatam to assume "the command of the northern division of the army, "having succeeded no further in accomplishing the ob-"jects of his mission, than in preventing the officers from "adopting any flagrant acts of outrage to authority during "his residence at Masulipatam."

The first charge is hardly less than a direct accusation of disobedience of orders. It is stated, that as it never was in the contemplation of Government to disband the European regiment, it was expected I would have taken the earliest opportunity to communicate to the men a distinct and public disavowal of that intention. In the succeeding paragraph I am accused of having adopted a course of proceeding entirely different from what Government had in view in deputing me; and I am positively charged *with "having abstained from making any direct "communication to the men."* My letter to Lieutenant-Colonel Barclay, of the 18th July, is a number of this dispatch, and has been printed with it. This letter contains the following passage: "You will satisfy Sir George "Barlow, that one of the first things that I did, after I "came on shore, was to satisfy the minds of the officers, "and, through them, of the men, of the intentions of Go-"vernment in ordering a party of marines from the corps; "*and you will see, by the enclosed extract from my "Journal, that I took the first good opportunity that "offered of* STATING THIS FACT *in the most public and "impressive manner to the whole regiment.*" I may ask, with great surprise and some indignation, Why the extract alluded to in this letter was not transmitted to the Honourable the Court of Directors? This extract was a copy of my speech made to the European regiment under arms on the 15th of July. The whole of this speech is in my Journal The following is a part of it.

"I consider it my duty to declare to you at this "moment, that it never was in the contemplation of Go- "vernment to *disband* or disperse this corps; and that it "never meant to employ any officer or man of the regiment "in any manner, or upon any service, but such as was "suited to the character of British soldiers; and which it, "of course, conceived both officers and men would be for- "ward to proceed upon."

Is it possible that any disavowal could be more distinct, or made in a more proper and military manner? Yet I am directly charged with *having abstained* from making any such communication to the *men!* It is possible a charge so completely unfounded may have originated in mistake or neglect: but where there exists, as on the present occasion, an evident desire to criminate; where the secret nature of the blow afforded no opportunity of defence; such mistake, even if proved, neither can nor ought to disarm honest resentment. It is too much to have a character, that has been obtained by the struggle of a whole life, assailed in such a manner. But the knowledge which the Governor of Fort St. George had of my proceeding, upon this point, was not limited to this communication through Lieutenant-Colonel Barclay. The day after my return to Madras, I read to him the whole of my Journal. It is true he did not pay much attention to it: and the little value he attached to the detail of my proceedings was the cause of my not loading my public report with a copy of its contents. I had neither received at that moment, nor at any subsequent period, the slightest official notice of even dissatisfaction; and the probability of my conduct being misrepresented to my superiors in

Vide Appendix.

England in the manner it has been, never once entered into my imagination.

In answer to the charge, " That I did not employ my " strenuous exertions to recall the men to a sense of their " duty, by impressing upon their minds the degree of " guilt and danger in which their officers, for purposes " entirely personal to themselves, had endeavoured to in- " volve them," I must reply in the most solemn manner, that I was not withheld from acting in the manner the Government here state they expected I would, merely because I had no orders to do so, but because I considered that such a proceeding would have had an operation directly opposite to all Sir George Barlow's intentions, as expressed when I left Madras. His desire then was, (as has already been shown,) to conciliate and reclaim the officers of the Company's army, not to render them desperate. I was particularly instructed to point their views to England, to persuade them by every effort to await the decision of the Honourable the Court of Directors, and to prevent their precipitating themselves into a guilt from which they could never retreat. Sir George Barlow ap peared satisfied I could effect this through the influence of my general character, and the power of reason, aided by the justice of the cause I had to support: and I most solemnly affirm, that if the Government of Madras desire to insinuate (as the substance of these passages in their letter would imply) that I acted contrary to the instructions of Sir George Barlow, communicated to me in private, that the charge is not founded in fact: and it is fortunate for me that the subsequent communications made by Sir George Barlow's Secretary, and all the circumstances of this case, completely corroborate and establish the truth of that unqualified assertion, which I have deemed it due to my character to make on this point. A letter from Lieutenant-Colonel Barclay*, dated the 12th of July, and written by

All the letters from this officer to me while I was at Masulipatam, are in the printed Correspondence.

the Governor's order, in reply to my communications from Masulipatam of the 4th, 5th, and 6th of July, in which I had required further orders, repeats nearly the same sentiments in the same language Sir George Barlow had used before I left Madras. "You cannot," he observes, "render a more acceptable service to the public interests, "than by the exertion of your influence and ability in "keeping the garrison of Masulipatam firm to their duty, "and *satisfying the officers* that it is not less for their interests than it is consistent with their duty, to await the "decision of the authorities in England on the several "questions which have occasioned so much agitation in "the minds of a considerable portion of the army of this "establishment."

The same officer wrote to me a short letter on the 20th of July, in which he repeats these sentiments, and concludes by stating, that the greatest service I could render my country, in the actual situation of affairs, was "to keep "the garrison in order, and bring the *minds of the officers* "*back to reason.*"

I was authorized, through the same channel, to proceed with the inquiry, (if I thought it advisable,) without waiting for my colleagues, reporting *the result*, *for the orders of Government*: and a discretion was vested in me to grant a pardon to the non-commissioned officers and privates of the garrison, if I should judge it necessary: but this was evidently in reference to the possible occurrence of a case of extreme emergency, which Colonel Barclay stated the Governor felt assured would not arise.

It will certainly not occur, on a perusal of what I have stated, that there existed the slightest ground for the Government of Fort St. George indulging those expectations which they have declared they did in their letter to the Secret Committee. Is it possible that they could, at the moment, have expected that an officer, instructed as I was, should have commenced his proceedings with "strenuous "exertions to excite the men against officers," whom he was directed to reclaim to their duty by the efforts of reason and argument? And when he had been commanded to carry on a military inquiry, in order to ascertain the nature and degree of the crimes of different individuals, was it reasonable to suppose he would disappoint the very object for which that was instituted, by a premature attempt to seize and bring ringleaders to trial, on whose guilt he was expressly told "it was his duty to report, "and to await the orders of Government?"

It is sufficiently obvious, from what has been stated, that when the Government of Fort St. George wrote those paragraphs (which have been quoted) to the Secret Committee, the object was more to preserve a character of consistence, than to give a correct view of the actual situation of affairs at the moment of the occurrence of those events which are described. The Government, in a subsequent part of the same dispatch, gives a more just account of the character of this proceeding. "We had hitherto," they observe, "continued to expect, that the firmness of our measures, "and the good sense of the officers of the army, would "have finally succeeded in restoring order: but we were "convinced, by the failure of Lieutenant-Colonel Malcolm's mission, by the addresses received from Hyderabad, and by the intelligence received from other "quarters, that it was necessary to calculate on the possibility of the officers proceeding to the last extremities "of rebellion; and to consider the means of preventing, "or finally of meeting, that arduous state of things. "The moderate course of conduct pursued by the Government, and which was founded on a favourable opinion "of the loyalty of the army, had failed; and we were "reduced to the alternative of making the concession "demanded by the officers, or subduing them by force."

Is it not evident from this paragraph alone, if other evidences were wanting, that the Government considered

One of the chief objects for which this proceeding was recommended and adopted, was to gain time.

my mission to Masulipatam as a proceeding which was calculated, by its moderation, to reclaim the officers to their duty; and in no degree whatever related to that course of measures which was subsequently adopted? A most desperate remedy was ultimately applied to the existing evils: and in having recourse to the expedient of exciting the men against their officers, and in impairing the strength if not destroying that link by which almost all are agreed we hold India, the Government of Fort St. George might perhaps be justified by the emergency of the moment; and the controlling authorities in England may be satisfied that this operation, however terrible, was necessary and politic; but assuredly (even if all this is granted) no person can believe that any authority but Government could adopt such a measure. It appears too much to have expected, that an officer sent to moderate the minds of a body of officers, and to reclaim them to their duty by argument and reason, should *(acting upon his own discretion, and without orders)* have adopted this desperate expedient; and that he should have commenced his efforts to persuade the officers to return to their duty, by exciting their men to throw off their authority.

The Government of Madras proceed to state, that it ascribes my failure to an apparent unreasonable and unwise forbearance and attention to the feelings of officers who had, by their acts of violence and aggression, forfeited all claims to consideration; that my time was occupied in negotiations with disorderly committees, and in fruitless attempts to bring officers back to their duty by argument. A reference is made to my reasons for this conduct, as stated in my letters * under date the 4th, 5th, and 6th of July. The measures which I recommended are there stated. These, the Government observed, "consisted of "a modified repeal of the orders of the 1st of May; the "restoration to the service, and to their appointments, of

* See Appendix.

"all the officers whom we had found it necessary to suspend or remove; with an intimation to the army, that "their claims to Bengal allowances would be brought to "the notice of the Honourable the Court of Directors." It is stated in the conclusion of this paragraph, that I returned to Madras, "having succeeded no further in "accomplishing the objects of my mission, than in preventing the officers from adopting any flagrant acts of "outrage to authority during my residence at Masulipatam." As my failure is ascribed to an apparent unreasonable and unwise attention to the feelings of officers who had by their acts of violence forfeited all claims to consideration, may it not be asked, What was the situation of these officers when I was deputed by Sir George Barlow with instructions to restore them to better feelings, and a juster sense of duty, by the efforts of reason and argument? Were they not in a state of outrageous mutiny? Their commanding officer, Lieutenant-Colonel Innes, had been placed under sentries, and it was hourly expected they would openly throw off even the show of obedience; and yet at such a period I received instructions from Sir George Barlow to use every effort of reason and argument to reclaim the officers to their duty. When I had, as appears from my Journal * and letters, in a great degree succeeded, having released Colonel Innes from his arrest, prevailed upon a mutinous garrison to abandon its design of immediately throwing off its allegiance, and of marching to Hyderabad, obtained from them a reluctant recognition of my authority, and was proceeding with the inquiry which I had been directed to make: when all these changes, I say, had been effected without *one concession*, by the force of that reason which I was directed to employ; and I had reported all that I had done; I received a letter from Colonel Barclay, written by order of Sir George Barlow, approving of my measures, desiring me to continue my

* Vide Appendix.

efforts to reclaim the officers, and to direct their attention to the decision of the authorities in England: and yet, when my success within the few days I was at Masulipatam had been as great as it was possible to expect such means could produce, (for changes in men's minds that are effected by reason and argument must be gradual,) I am accused, in a secret dispatch to my superiors in England, of having failed in my mission, from a forbearance, which, though subsequently termed unreasonable and unwise, I have shown Sir George Barlow deemed, or professed to deem, at the moment of my departure from Madras, wise and politic; and from an attention to the feelings of those very officers, to whose feelings and reason, when their crimes were at the greatest height, I had been directed, by the verbal instructions of Sir George Barlow, *and the letters* of his secretary, to address myself.

It is stated, that my time was occupied in communication with disorderly committees. To this I reply, that I never recognised any committee in any public or official manner that could either compromise my own authority, or commit the dignity of Government. I communicated, it is true, chiefly with those officers who, from their rank or ability, appeared to have most influence over the rest. Not to have done so, would have been to neglect the employment of those means to which I have shown Sir George Barlow exclusively trusted for my success. I learnt, that there existed a garrison committee, of which every officer was a member, and which could never meet without danger of a mutiny that in its consequences would have precipitated a rupture between the Government and most other parts of the army: an extreme which it was my constant labour to retard, if I could not altogether avert. This committee I endeavoured, by my influence with the senior and more reflecting officers of the garrison, to dissolve; and I considered my success in this point as a great step towards the restoration of order. The control of the proceedings of the whole became vested in a few senior officers of comparative moderation, whose minds were more accessible to reason, and whose small numbers rendered them less liable to those violent impressions which produce such mischief in large and turbulent meetings But all the communications I ever had, either directly or indirectly, with any individual or bodies of officers at Masulipatam, are stated in my journal: and, it will be seen from that, I never made the slightest concession to the repeated demands of the officers of that garrison. That my proceedings were not such as is prescribed by an observation of the regular course of military discipline there can be no doubt: but Government had itself decided that question. They had refrained (for the reasons stated in the dispatch to which I have so often referred) from resorting to the usual means, the employment of force for quelling the mutiny at Masulipatam. I was deputed on what is termed in this very dispatch *a mission*, (a word in itself including a volume,) in order that I might reclaim to duty, by the efforts of reason and argument, the officers of a garrison which were known to be almost to a man unanimously bent on mutiny and opposition to authority; and yet I am subsequently condemned by the Government that sent me, for having used the only means by which it was possible I could accomplish that object.

The statement made in the same paragraph of this dispatch regarding the character of those measures which I recommended, with a view of terminating the agitation of the army, will, I am assured, not be considered as either fair or liberal, by any person who gives an attentive perusal to my secret and confidential letter to Sir George Barlow upon that subject. I saw, immediately after my arrival at Masulipatam, that some conciliatory measures must be instantly adopted by Government, if it intended to avoid the desperate extreme of a contest with its own army. A contest which, it will be recollected, I never doubted would early terminate in favour of the former: but success, I was convinced, would bring dangers of a hundred fold greater magnitude than any that could result from issuing the order that I recommended.

On the succeeding day I wrote another letter†, which contained the following paragraph:

"I can think of no improvement to this order, except "you conceive the great object of avoiding hostilities "would justify the following addition to it. 'Govern- "ment received a representation from a number of the "officers of the coast army, in which they solicit the "equalization of their allowances with those of the offi- "cers of the Bengal army: This is a subject, the con- "sideration of which must exclusively rest with the "Honourable the Court of Directors, under whose notice "this application will, *in course,* be brought, and by "whose decision it will be the duty of the officers of the "coast army to abide.'"

I may ask, Whether the order I suggested in my letter of the 5th of July justifies the assertion in the letter from the Madras Government, that I recommended "the resto- "ration to the service and their appointments of all the "officers the Government had removed." The terms of the order I suggested were only, that *in the full confidence* that the officers of the coast would immediately abandon their proceedings, Government would *recommend* the *offi- cers suspended to the Court of Directors*. That it restored Colonels Bell and Chalmers to command, from which they had been removed, and also one or two staff officers who were in a similar predicament. There is assuredly a wide difference between the immediate restoration of all the offi- cers suspended from the service, and the conditional pro- mise of a favourable recommendation to that authority by which, under every circumstance, the fate of these officers must have been decided. With respect to Colonel Bell, I conscientiously believed at the moment, from what I

See a copy of that order in the Appendix, in a letter to Sir George Barlow, dated 5th July.

† See Appendix.

knew of the case of that valuable officer, that Sir George Barlow would not be reluctant to consent to his restoration; and with regard to that of Colonel Chalmers and one or two others in nearly similar predicaments, I conceived that if any measure of this kind was adopted, it should be as complete as it was possible to make it, without affecting the principle which was to carry *conciliation in act* (words, after what had passed, could be of little or no avail) as far as was possible, without serious injury to the authority and dignity of Government. It was this consideration which led to the communication already quoted from my letter of the 6th of July regarding the first Memorial forwarded by General McDowall. What I recommended was nothing more than what had, I believe, been done as an act of course, and was stated in a mode which, though conciliatory, reminded the army of their duty, and gave them no reason to believe more, than that the Court of Directors *would see* the document in question. I think at this moment, as I did at that in which I recommended this measure, that nothing could have been more fortunate than its adoption. I know I differ on this point from very high authorities, who believe that any concessions, (and such they would appear to deem *every act* of conciliation,) however modified and corrected, would have been ruinous to Government: but, in spite of these imposing opinions , I

I always thought, and always must think, that there is a wide difference between the seditious combination of a body of officers and a mutiny of soldiers, and that the two cases require a distinct treatment. With the latter there can hardly be two modes of proceeding; with the former there may be various, and all equally safe. They may be restored by the influence of reason, and subdued by the operation of their own feelings. Their minds may be reclaimed by many modes that could not be applied to their men; and there is, in the worst extremes, a character in their opposition that admits more of the application of such remedies than the mad and instinctive action of a mutinous soldiery. These two cases were certainly confounded at Madras; and most of the evils that arose may be imputed to the fallacy of treating a seditious combination of officers as a mutiny of soldiers.

must ask reflecting men to look near the subject, to examine the evil which this measure could have produced, consider the ills that were at that moment to be expected, and to think on those that have resulted from the complete success to authority that the most sanguine could have anticipated, and then to pronounce their cool and deliberate judgment. There certainly could be no apprehension entertained that this order would have strengthened, to any purpose of immediate violence or opposition, the discontented and turbulent: but the danger stated is, that those would have deemed it a victory. Let us for a moment suppose they had been led, by their first feelings of joy at their escape from a punishment which they had merited, to have considered it as such, what permanent effect could such a feeling produce? what had they gained? *Nothing*. The fate of the officers who had been suspended remained to be decided by the Directors; with whom it must, under all circumstances, ultimately rest. Their Memorial for an increase of allowances was to be brought before the same body, but without even a promise from Government of any recommendation. There was an end to their combinations and committees , and, with them, to all those threats they had thrown out against the local Government, which, it was evident, would acquire such a vast accession of strength by the spirit of moderation and conciliation which it had shown, as would fully enable it to enforce the most severe discipline, and particularly in all cases which were attended with a danger of the recurrence of evils of a similar character to those it had so recently encountered. The majority, indeed, of the officers of the army, and all the most re-

The danger that had been incurred was sufficient to authorize Government to take the most decisive measures to guard against the revival of such combinations against authority: and though numbers who might have merited punishment had escaped, *not one object of benefit to either individuals or the army at large had been attained*; and it is therefore quite extravagant to assert such a termination could ever have tended to encourage future proceedings of a similar nature.

spectable, had seen at this moment the desperate situation into which they had unwarily suffered themselves to be led. They would have had no sentiments but those of gratitude to a Government, whose consideration had presented them with the means of escape. All these would, if such an indulgence had been shown to their errors, have ranged themselves with enthusiasm on the side of Government, and would have been the most forward to retrieve the character of the service, by the punishment of those whom a hardened spirit of disaffection and turbulence had led to continue in opposition. That such a class would also have remained, there is no doubt; and Government might have been satisfied, at the moment this measure was taken, that future punishments would have corrected any erroneous opinions regarding the true motives that had induced so generous and politic a proceeding.

The situation of affairs at the period stated was such, that though there could be little doubt of the ultimate success of Government even under the violent course it pursued; yet that did not appear likely to be attained, if extremes were resorted to, without bloodshed. His Majesty's regiments at Hyderabad* and Travancore would be, if a contest was precipitated, in the utmost danger; and if the combat between our European and native troops had once commenced, feelings would have been instantly engendered, the dreadful action of which no man could calculate. That these results were averted, was owing to a variety of causes, very little, if at all, connected with either the foresight or vigour of the Government of Fort St. George.

* The account of what occurred at this station on the day General Close made the noble effort he did to carry the orders of the Government of Madras into execution, shows the desperate hazard that was incurred. If, says an officer of high rank, during the period that between four and five thousand troops were in a state of mutinous violence and uproar, "one musket had gone off by accident, not a man of his Majesty's 33d "regiment would have been left alive, and a general massacre of almost "all Europeans would have been the most certain result."

But, passing over what was likely to be the probable results of the desperate extreme to which the Government of Fort St. George had resort, (though it is by a consideration of these results that the merit of my suggestions should be tried,) let us contemplate what has occurred, from the most favourable issue that could have been anticipated. The officers of the coast army must long continue to feel that degradation which they have endured. Years must elapse before the action of this feeling will cease to produce disunion and discontent in that establishment. But these are comparatively light considerations, as all questions must be, connected with a body of men over whom we must always have such strong ties and efficient control as the European officers of our armies in India. It is the firm allegiance and continued obedience of the natives of which the strength of those armies is composed, which forms by far the most important principle in our government of this great Empire. This can never be denied: and it is as true, that in that almost religious respect with which the sepoy of India has hitherto regarded his European officer, consisted what has been always deemed the chief link of this great chain of duty and obedience. That link (as far as relates to the sepoys of the coast establishment) has, if not broken, been greatly shattered and impaired. A temporary object of importance, no doubt, has been gained by a sacrifice of one a thousand times the value of the object. The dignity of the local Government of Fort St. George has been saved from an imputation of weakness, by a measure which threatens the most serious danger to the future safety of our whole empire in India. An evil, for which there were many and certain remedies, has been averted, by incurring one, the progress of which (from its character,) cannot be

* No consideration of this question can be local or limited. If a successful example of disobedience or rebellion was exhibited by our native troops on the Madras establishment, its baneful effects would not be limited to that part of our possessions.

calculated; which is, from its nature, irremediable; and of which we know nothing, except that it is efficient to our destruction.

The Government of Fort St. George appear resolved to withhold the expression of their sense of that benefit which the substance of their dispatch obviously shows flowed from my observation and conduct. Sir George Barlow, through his secretary, Lieutenant-Colonel Barclay, to me, under date the 12th of July, states, that, " *in consequence of the* " *information which I had communicated" from* Masulipatam, he had ordered the assembling of a considerable force near Madras; and it is to this precautionary measure, adopted upon my information, to which the Government of Madras ascribes in a great degree the success of its subsequent proceedings: and it seems also to have entirely escaped the recollection of the Government, that if I had not, by my exertions, reclaimed the garrison of Masulipatam from their design of marching to join the Hyderabad force, and prevented from the 4th till the 22d of July their committing any outrage, that a great part of the army would, during that eventful period, have been precipitated into a rupture before the Government had time for executing any plan for the defeat of their designs. I do not mention these circumstances with a view of claiming any merit from my exertions at that period; but to show that the same principle, which led to an unfounded insinuation against my character, has caused an omission of every fact that could bring my services to the favourable notice of my superiors.

I shall resume my narrative, and state shortly what share I had in the transactions at Madras, from my return from Masulipatam till the arrival of Lord Minto at that settlement.

I have already stated that Sir George Barlow directed me, before I went to Masulipatam, to write the draft of a letter to the commanding officers at Hyderabad and Jaulnah, and had approved of what I had written. I had carried a copy of that draft to Masulipatam, and had, on my first violent discussion with the officers of that garrison, adduced it as a proof of the moderation and temper with which the Governor had acted. In a short period, however, it appeared that no such document had reached Hyderabad, and I was exposed to the charge of intended deception. I addressed a note to Colonel Barclay the day after I arrived at Madras, stating this fact, and begged that he would, by his answer, enable me to repel such a charge . I received the following reply, dated Fort St. George, 28th July 1809.

" Dear Malcolm,

" I have just received your note of " this date. I recollect perfectly well, that before your " embarkation for Masulipatam you put into my hands, " to be delivered to Sir George Barlow, a paper in the " form of a draft of a letter to be written to Colonel Mon- " tresor, on the subject of addresses from the Hyderabad " subsidiary force. I delivered the paper according to " your desire. I know that Sir George Barlow did not " approve of it; and I believe that no letter of the nature " of it was sent to Colonel Montresor.

" I remain, &c. &c.

(Signed) " R. BARCLAY."

I spoke to Colonel Barclay before I wrote upon this subject, and he said he would show my note to Sir G. Barlow, and obtain me an answer that would vindicate my character from the charge to which the Governor's change of resolution had made me liable. This circumstance left me without a doubt that the cautious reply I received from that officer was by the direction of Sir G. Barlow. Indeed, I was satisfied that this excellent and respectable officer, for whom I have always entertained the same sentiments of esteem and friendship, never acted in any part of those transactions, in which his name appears, *but by the specific instructions or orders of the Governor*.

Greatly surprised at this answer, I wrote the following note:

" Dear Barclay,

" There must be a mistake, as the
" draft I gave you was written, by direction of Sir George
" Barlow, from a memorandum now in my possession,
" which I had read to Sir George not half an hour before,
" and of which he at that moment approved, or he would
" not have desired me to put it in the shape of a letter.
" I beg the nature of the request I made in my note of
" yesterday may not be misunderstood. I am aware Sir
" George Barlow, when he asked my opinion on the
" question of the reply to be made to the representation
" from the Hyderabad force, might, even if he approved
" my suggestion at the moment, be led by a thousand con-
" siderations to alter his sentiments before the tappal was
" dispatched; but as I sailed for Masulipatam under the
" impression that no change had occurred in his opinion,
" and made use of the information I had upon the subject,
" to satisfy misguided men that they were in error regard-
" ing his disposition towards them, and by doing so have
" subjected myself to a charge of *intended deception*, I
" was naturally anxious to clear my character from this
" imputation; and the circumstances were evidently such,
" that it appeared in my mind I would be enabled to do
" so without the slightest embarrassment to either you or
" Sir George Barlow. If, indeed, i had not been satisfied
" of this, I should never have written, at a moment like
" the present, upon such a subject. Your note conveys
" no idea but that I had, without any previous communi-
" cation with Sir George Barlow, sent a draft of a letter
" to him through you, of which he disapproved; and so
" far from answering the object for which it was solicited,

“ could make no impression but that my assertions were “ founded on an ill-grounded presumption of my possess- “ ing an influence over the judgment of Sir G. Barlow. “ *This, you must be aware, is exactly opposite to the cir-* “ *cumstances of the case, as I have stated them to you at* “ *the period of their occurrence*; for I told you it was by “ desire of Sir George Barlow I gave you the draft.

“ I have felt it due to myself to say so much, but am “ not desirous a word more should pass on the subject. “ I trust it never has and never can be supposed, that I “ could either in word or deed do any thing that could “ occasion the slightest embarrassment upon any question, “ much less upon one of so personal a nature.

“ Your's sincerely,

(Signed) “ JOHN MALCOLM.”

To this communication I received the following more satisfactory reply:

“ Dear Malcolm,

“ I have been so busy for the last two “ days, that I could not refer to the answer which I wrote “ on the 28th ultimo to your letter of that date, respecting “ the draft of the letter which you gave me for Sir George “ Barlow previous to your embarkation for Masulipatam.

“ I now find that it is not mentioned in that answer that “ you had prepared the draft at Sir George Barlow's de- “ sire, after a long conversation with him on the subject; “ *but I recollect perfectly well that you told me so when* “ *you gave me the draft.*

“ I remain, &c. &c.

(Signed) “ R. BARCLAY,
“ M. S.”

“ Fort St. George,
1st August, 1809.”

This trifling but irritating circumstance confirmed me in the resolution I had taken regarding my own conduct. I had come from Bombay with the intention of joining my station at Mysore; but I had received, when at Masulipatam, a letter from Lord Minto reappointing me to Persia; and I had, since I reached Madras, been directed by a letter from his Lordship, under date the 15th of July, to await his arrival at that place. With such orders I could only offer my service as a volunteer to Sir George Barlow; and I had little encouragement to do that. He had, it is true, at the interview I had on the 27th, expressed in a cold manner his wish that I should go to Mysore; but that wish had never been repeated: he had made no further communication to me since my return; nor had I even been required to give that information which he knew I possessed. Under such circumstances, I felt that it was my duty to obey the orders of the Governor-General, and not to intrude my voluntary services when they were evidently not sought. In consequence of this determination I addressed a private letter to Sir George Barlow on the 1st of August; in which, after explaining very fully the sentiments by which my conduct was regulated, I offered the following observations on what had passed, and what might be expected from the measure he had adopted:

"You are no stranger to that enthusiasm with which I "embarked in the present scene: and, whatever has been "my success, I am assured that you are satisfied I have "not been deficient in zeal in the exertion of my humble "endeavours to reclaim my brother officers to temper and "to the path of duty: and I indulged, to the very moment "of my arrival at Madras from Masulipatam, a hope that "this great object of your solicitude would be effected "without having recourse to coercive measures; or at "least that a great proportion of the officers of the Company's army (including almost all who had weight and "influence with the men) would be recovered, and that

" the early submission of the rest would have been a certain consequence of the return of their seniors to their duty.

" The highly criminal violence of the force at Hyderabad, which is known to the whole army to be guided by weak and wrong-headed men, has unfortunately precipitated a very different issue to that which I was so sanguine as to expect. That force has declared that they speak the sentiments of the whole, or at least those of a great proportion of the Madras army; though it is evident, at the moment they made such an assertion, they could not have received an answer from any station to that absurd paper which they term an *Ultimatum*, which they have had the audacity to forward to Government; but which, I conscientiously believe, would, if it had been publicly promulgated, have been disowned and disclaimed by great numbers of the senior and most respectable officers at every station in the army. I can speak positively with regard to some, indeed all of the senior officers of the garrison of Masulipatam upon this subject, and they have lately been considered as the most violent of the whole. I am far from meaning (such meaning would, indeed, be as contrary to that high respect I have ever entertained for your character, as to the duties of my situation) to offer even an opinion on the wisdom and policy of that step which Government has lately adopted with the Company's officers of this establishment. The test these were required to sign was, as far as I understood it, a mere repetition of the obligations of the commission that every one of them held; and the only rational objection that could be made to it by men who were devoted to their duty, and who had never deviated from it in thought, word, or deed, was, that it was unnecessary; that it was, with regard to them at least, an act of supererogation, and one that had a taint of suspicion in it. These were, indeed, the feelings that passed

" in my mind when this paper was first put into my " hands; but they were instantly subdued by a paramount " sense of public duty; and I signed it to show (as far as " my example could show) my perfect acquiescence in a " measure which the Government I served had thought " proper to adopt: but I am satisfied it was not the terms " of this paper which led the great majority of the Com- " pany's officers both in camp and at the Mount, and in " the garrison, to refuse their signatures; it was the man- " ner in which it was presented, and the circumstances " by which the whole proceeding was accompanied. " The minds of the most honourable, and of those most " attached to Government and to their Country, revolted " more at the mode than the substance of the act: they " felt (perhaps erroneously) that they were disgraced, " because the manner in which their consent was asked " showed they were not in the least trusted: and this was, " I am assured, one of the chief causes of their almost " general rejection of this proposed test of fidelity. It " appears to me of the greatest importance that you " should be aware of every feeling that this proceeding " excited; and it is in discharge of the duties of that " friendship with which you have ever honoured me " that I have stated my sentiments so freely upon this " subject. I am very intimately acquainted with a great " number of the officers of whom I speak: some of them " would, I am certain, have given their lives for Govern- " ment at the very moment they refused to give a pledge " which they thought, from the mode in which it was " proposed, reflected upon their honour; and others, who " had unfortunately gone to a certain extent in the late " culpable and unmilitary proceedings, but who viewed " the criminal excesses of some of their brother officers " with undisguised horror and indignation, would, I am " assured, if it had been possible for Government to have " pardoned what was past, and to have expressed, in in- " dulgent language, its kind intentions for the future,

" have been the most forward in their efforts to punish
" those who, by an unwarrantable perseverance in a guilty
" career, merited all the wrath of the state : but, unfortu-
" nately, (though such an intention, I am assured, never
" entered into your mind,) an almost general sentiment
" prevailed, that it was meant the service should be
" destroyed by the first blow, and that all were therefore
" included in one general mass, as just objects of suspicion
" and disgrace.

" I am far from defending such an interpretation of this
" measure of Government; I have only stated what I
" consider to be the fact, and explained, as far as I could,
" those causes by which I believe it to have been pro-
" duced : their operation is, I fear, now almost irremedi-
" able, and events must take their course. I know (and
" my personal conduct has proved it,) that my brother
" officers are deeply wrong ; and I am quite heart-broken
" when I reflect on the consequences to themselves and
" country which the guilt of some of them is likely to
" produce. I need not assure you of my sincere happi-
" ness at the success which has hitherto attended the exe-
" cution of the measure you have adopted, and I
" anxiously hope it may meet with no opposition. I
" have never doubted the success of this measure, if it was
" resorted to, as far as related to the accomplishment of
" its immediate object; and I most earnestly pray that
" my judgment may have deceived me with regard to the
" collateral and remote consequences by which I have
" always deemed it likely to be attended."

The only reply I received to this communication, was by a note from Colonel Barclay, under date the 2d of August, to acquaint me, that, for the reasons I had stated, " Sir George Barlow would not press me to go to Mysore, " and that it was the Governor's intention to reply to the " other parts of my letter at more leisure." He never, however, condescended to make such a reply, or indeed to honour me with any subsequent communication whatever, either personally, or through the medium of any of his staff: and an event occurred sometime afterwards, which produced such irritation upon his mind, as to make him deny me the common civilities due to an officer in my public station. Some time after my return to Madras, an address* from the inhabitants of Madras to Sir George Barlow was drawn up, and sent in circulation. This address was said to have originated with a staff officer of rank. None of the usual forms of convening the inhabitants had taken place; and the mode adopted to obtain signatures was still more extraordinary than this glaring departure from common usage. Gentlemen of the first respectability in the civil service informed me, that when they had testified an aversion to sign this address unless parts of it were modified, they had received such plain intimations regarding the consequences with which their refusal would be attended, as left them in no doubt but that they must either sacrifice their opinions, or bring immediate distress, and perhaps final ruin, upon themselves and their families. Under these circumstances some had signed; while others had actually absented themselves for days from their own houses, to escape the painful importunities to which they were exposed. It is necessary here to state, that almost all ranks were ready at this moment to come forward with a public declaration of duty and attachment to Government, and of their readiness to sacrifice their lives and fortunes in its defence; but a strong objection was entertained by many to that part of the circulated address which cast reflections upon that body of officers who had embraced the alternative of retiring for a period from their duty, rather than sign the test which Government had proposed. It was said, and with great truth, that at the moment when Government professed its desire to reclaim these officers to a more active allegiance, nothing could be more unwise and useless than exasperat-

* See a copy of this in the Appendix.

ing their minds to a sullen perseverance in error, by an abuse of them in an address signed by a few civil and military inhabitants of Madras; and that it was perfectly evident such an expression of sentiment could only have the effect of widening a breach it was most desirable to close, and of creating (by exciting discussion) further dissensions and difference of opinion among those of whose devoted attachment to Government there could be no doubt. Such were my own sentiments regarding this address: and while I foresaw the mischief it was calculated to produce, I could divine no possible good from its agitation. It was sent for my signature, with the following note from Colonel Leith:

"The accompanying address is submitted to Lieute-
" nant-Colonel Malcolm for his consideration, which, as
" soon as he is done with, it is requested he will return to
" the bearer."

To this I immediately sent an answer, as follows:

" Lieutenant-Colonel Malcolm returns the address to
" Lieutenant-Colonel Leith. He has not signed it, for
" reasons very foreign to any want of respect and regard
" for Sir George Barlow, or of duty, obedience, and
" attachment to that constituted authority of his country
" under which he is placed."

I cannot recollect that I ever in my life took a step in which my mind was more decided respecting its propriety, on every public and private principle, than upon this occasion. I considered the address, both from the irregular mode in which it was brought forward, the unbecoming means resorted to in order to obtain signatures, and the expressions contained in it, as an unwise measure, which had originated in that spirit of undistinguishing violence which I conscientiously believed had been the chief means of producing a crisis that this act was calculated to inflame It did not appear to my mind to be attended with the slightest benefit, for it brought no new friends to Government: and though it could not shake the attachment to the legitimate authority of their country of any persons whose principles were fixed, its tendency was to excite jealousy and division among those who were most warmly attached to order and Government: and among these, however actuated by a sense of public duty, it was natural that a difference of *private opinion* should exist. Some were, no doubt, more disposed than others to approve violent and unqualified proceedings, or perhaps less disposed to maintain that independence of mind which no man should ever be censured for maintaining upon such points; otherwise addresses of this stamp would not only lose their value, but become tests of the most odious and invidious nature that a tyrannic Government could invent, to degrade or alienate the minds of its subjects.

I certainly was most reluctant to believe that this measure had Sir George Barlow's sanction: it seemed to me of a character opposite to all the principles and habits of his life: nor could I forget those grounds which he had assumed when he recently refused to permit me to frame an address of a very opposite tendency, and one that would, in all probability, have prevented those evils which this seemed calculated to inflame. I never was more surprised than when (some days subsequent to my note to Colonel Leith) I was informed by a confidential officer of the Governor's staff, to whom I mentioned what I had done, and the reasons by which I was actuated, that the address, from the first, had the Governor's complete sanction and approbation.

In closing this subject, it may be necessary to state, that this address, after all the unbecoming efforts that were used to obtain signatures, had only fifty-seven names affixed to it; among which, twenty-four only were civilians and inhabitants of Madras: the remainder were officers of his Majesty's service, with a few of the staff of the Company's army. If all those who did not sign it were not actually considered as disaffected, they were deemed by those whom this measure had formed into a party, as lukewarm in the public cause. This species of injustice is too common to such times, to afford any individual a right of complaint; but there should be a difference between the momentary feeling of a violent party during a period of commotion, and the deliberate sentiments of a public ruler. I have already mentioned, that the crime of having presumed, though in the most respectful manner, to act conformably to the dictates of my own judgment on a question which was referred to me as a private individual, subjected me, at the moment, to the loss of those civilities from Sir George Barlow to which I had a right from my public station; and I did not require the evidence I have now obtained, from the publication of the letter from the Government of Madras to the Secret Committee, to satisfy my mind that my character has since had to war with all the weight that belongs to the influence and opinion of Sir George Barlow: but, great as this odds may appear to many, it can excite no apprehension in a mind fortified as mine is by a conscious sense of never having deviated from the path of private rectitude, or public duty.

Though, subsequent to this transaction, all personal intercourse between Sir George Barlow and me had ceased, I could not look with indifference on the events that occurred; and when the mad desperation of the officers of the two corps which marched from Chittledroog to proceed to Seringapatam led to an action, I thought the opportunity favourable to close this horrid scene in a manner every way suited to the dignity of Government. I first communicated my sentiments upon this point to Lieutenant-Colonel Barclay, and afterwards ventured to address the following note to Sir George Barlow, expecting that the importance of the subject, and a consideration of former acquaintance and regard, would at least obtain a pardon for such a liberty.

"Dear Sir,

"I wrote a note to Colonel Barclay some hours "ago, which he informed me he sent to you for perusal. "I have since received a letter from Masulipatam, at

" which place they are between hope and despair; but
" have refrained from further guilt, and mean to refrain,
" unless called upon by those who have now, thank God!
" shown them an example of returning to their duty. I
" am assured you will not blame that extreme anxiety
" which makes me intrude, unasked, my opinion at a
" moment like the present. I have, I am satisfied, the
" fullest information of the real temper of this army at this
" present period; and, if I am not the most deceived man
" in the world, there is an opportunity given, by the con-
" duct of the Hyderabad force*, which enables you to
" combine the immediate and complete settlement of these
" afflicting troubles with the advancement of the reputa-
" tion, power, and dignity, of Government. I am aware
" of the very deep guilt into which almost all have gone;
" some in intention, others in act: but the force at Hyder-
" abad, who, since the 1st of May, have been the cause
" of all the present evils, and who lately insulted Govern-
" ment with demands, are now supplicating clemency: a
" dreadful † example has occurred in Mysore, which will
" make a lasting impression on both officers and sepoys,
" of the horrors to which such illegal combinations lead.
" If it were possible to close the scene here, an impression
" must be made that will for ever prevent the repetition of
" such crimes; and the effect of shame and contrition,
" which the clemency and magnanimity of Government
" must produce, will have more effect upon the minds of
" liberal men than twenty examples.. Men's minds will
" be at once reclaimed, and they will be fixed in their
" attachment by a better motive than fear. But this is
" not all. The officers at Hyderabad, like those of other
" stations, act at the present crisis entirely from the im-
" pulse of passion and feeling; and they fly, as I have

The officers of that force had signed the test.

† It was considered, at the moment when this note was written, that almost the whole of the two corps from Chittledroog had been destroyed.

" witnessed, from one extreme to another, with a facility " that is not to be credited by persons under the influence " of calm reason. Such persons can never be depended " upon, whatever pledges they make, while any strong " causes of agitation remain: and no act, therefore, which " does not embrace the whole, can give that complete " security and tranquillity which is the object of desire. " If a single question of irritation and inflammation be " left, it is a spark which may again create a general ex- " plosion.

" You will, I am assured, pardon this communication. " Nothing could have induced me to the freedom, but a " conviction that this is one of those happy moments " when all the dangers that threaten us may be dissipated. " If you can, on the grounds of your granting that " clemency to supplication, which you never would to " demand; of military justice being satisfied, and the " army lessoned, in the dreadful example that has been " made in Mysore; and of your thinking it not deroga- " tory, at such a moment, to grant a general amnesty, " and to bury the past in oblivion: desiring all those who " mean to perform their duty to join their corps, and " those who do not, to consider themselves out of the ser- " vice; and proclaiming every man a traitor, and liable " to immediate military execution, who opposes legal " authority one hour after the receipt of this order, I will " answer with my life for the immediate re-establishment " of the public authority on more secure grounds than it " perhaps ever rested. Such an act as this will, I am " assured, while it advances the fame and dignity of " Government, raise your own reputation in the highest " degree; and you will receive, as you will merit, the " blessings of thousands, with the applause of your " country.

" I have perhaps already said too much upon this " subject; and I could adduce many more equally for- " cible reasons to those I have urged; but I shall not

" trouble you further. If you think the suggestions I
" have offered worthy of any attention, I shall attend
" you, and state them. With regard to the success of
" this measure I cannot have a doubt. If all did not im-
" mediately submit, they would be completely disunited:
" and those that ventured to oppose (if there were any
" such), would be the proper objects for example.

" I am, with great respect,

" Your obedient servant,

(Signed) " JOHN MALCOLM."

The receipt of this note was not even acknowledged; and it was, of course, the last communication I made to Sir George Barlow. When Lord Minto arrived at Madras, I laid every part of my conduct before him. I gave him every information I could regarding the actual state of affairs; and submitted with freedom my sentiments of those principles which should govern his final judgment on the important points that remained for his decision. He expressed no dissatisfaction at my conduct; he thanked me for my information; and though he differed with me in many of the opinions I stated, he did not condemn me for that difference: on the contrary, he appeared pleased with the liberty I took in offering my advice with such boldness and freedom. The whole of the manner, as well as the substance of the conduct, which this able and virtuous nobleman observed towards me on this occasion, had the effect of reconciling my mind to further exertions in the public service; from which, I confess, it was, before his arrival, much, if not wholly alienated. I had been employed, as I have shown, in a confidential manner, without being trusted. I had been deputed on a delicate and arduous mission, and recommended to pursue a system which mixed firmness with conciliation, while it proposed to reclaim by reason more than by terror; and before any time was given for the operation of the measures I had taken, a new course was adopted, grounded *on coercion* alone: and because I had not by inspiration divined that such would be the ultimate result, I now discover that I have been most unjustly censured, as disappointing the expectations of the Government: and it has been insinuated (a direct charge would have been too bold) that I acted contrary to orders. I trust I have refuted every charge of this nature: and if some should continue to think I have committed errors; none, I am assured, can accuse me of crimes. Let it be recollected that I was placed, throughout all the transactions I have described, in a most painful and difficult situation. I had no prescribed or distinct duty to perform; I was called upon by Sir G. Barlow to exert, in the manner I thought best adapted to the end, all the influence of my character to reclaim men with whom he thought I had great weight; and he appeared for a period to give me his confidence, and to trust implicitly to my discretion and judgment. I was all along sensible to the full danger of the situation in which I placed myself; but was too earnest in the cause to attend to prudence: and I may conscientiously add, that I never was more assured of meeting approbation from Sir George Barlow than at that moment when I found myself estranged from all share in his confidence, and treated with the most pointed neglect. But I had myself to reproach. I should certainly have foreseen that my efforts would have been useless, when combined with a system of measures to which they bore little or no affinity; and I was (I must confess it,) wrong in supposing, for a moment, that my advice, or any arguments I could adduce, could, under any circumstances, permanently divert the Governor of Fort St. George into a course that mixed feeling, and consideration for human failings, with the established maxims of his ordinary rule. I should have known better; and in fact I did, as my letters * before I went to Madras prove:

* Vide letters to Lords Wellesley and Wellington, pages 64, 65.

but, when on the spot, my heart conquered my head, and I tried an impossibility: but I never shall regret the attempt, nor blush for having recommended principles of action that are congenial to the best feelings of human nature, that are calculated to make Government an object of rational attachment, and to give the mind a generous pride in submission and obedience; and which, so far from being of dangerous example, and subversive of order, are familiar in the practice to every free state, and have never been rejected in the most despotic, when such have been governed by great and wise rules.

APPENDIX.

No. I.

Copies of Letters from Lieutenant-Colonel MALCOLM *during his Stay at Masulipatam.*

TO SIR GEORGE BARLOW

Masulipatam, 4th July, 1809.

DEAR SIR,

I ARRIVED here early this morning. Nothing can be worse than the state in which matters were. Major Storey seems a weak man, and the garrison was commanded by a committee of violent spirited young men. They deliberated, after my arrival, on the measures they were to pursue; and were at first, I am assured, disposed to resist my authority: they next made a demand of an act of amnesty for all late proceedings in the garrison of Masulipatam. This, I told them, it was quite impossible for me to grant; that a regular military proceeding had been instituted, to inquire into late proceedings; and that I could declare, it was the intention of Government to order a court martial to try any person this court thought ought to be tried; but I could say no more. They had, I found, pledged themselves most deeply to resist Government, to almost all the stations in the army*, and had

* I have not complete evidence of this fact.

received the strongest assurances of support from Hyderabad; and I believe a movement towards that quarter was intended in a day or two. The public avowal of their determination to resist Government made them feel reluctant to relax their opposition; and their fear of suffering for what has past, rendered them quite desperate. They, however, after a conference of some hours, became more reasonable, and professed their obedience to my authority, and their acquiescence in the inquiry that had been ordered. I issued the general orders, and directed the instant release of Lieutenant-Colonel Innes from arrest. I saw him. He is no doubt a very good, but he is a weak man. He feels naturally very indignant at what has passed, but will be moderate in his conduct. I could have had no idea of the length to which matters have proceeded, before to-day. An organized opposition to Government was to have commenced as the day after to-morrow; and, in the present temper of men, I know not if that event can be avoided. Nothing can be so unfortunate as the occurrences of the mutiny here, as numbers have been hurried into guilt, from which they see no escape but in all being equally involved. This is a melancholy state to have minds in. I have certainly succeeded in making them abandon their violent measures for the moment; but a relapse is to be apprehended; particularly as it would appear difficult, if not impossible, to tranquillize them by an act of amnesty. What am I to do, in case of an extreme? The combination is general. Excuse this hurried note. I have not a moment.

I am, with great respect,

Your obedient servant,

(Signed) JOHN MALCOLM.

TO SIR GEORGE BARLOW.

Masulipatam, 5th July, 1809.

DEAR SIR,

I WROTE you a hurried letter last night. I have since come to the knowledge of many additional facts, and have had some time to reflect on what I have seen and heard; and I should be as wanting in my duty to you as to my country, if I was withheld, by any motive whatever, in stating my sentiments in the most undisguised manner on the present state of affairs: and whether you coincide in my opinion or not, you can have no doubt regarding those motives that lead me to express, in that sacred confidence, which your knowledge of my character authorizes me to use, the conviction of my judgment on the steps necessary to be taken upon the present unfortunate crisis.

I have now seen the concerted plans of almost the whole of the army against the authority of Government; and can say, with almost an assurance that I am correct, that there is not one Company's corps, from Cape Comorin to Ganjam, that is not implicated in the general guilt, and that is not pledged to rise against Government, unless what they deem their grievances are redressed. Be assured, that no commanding officer, whatever they may write, has any real authority over their corps*: and though in some places (where there are King's regiments) they are more guarded, their resolution is the same; and they mean to act, the moment the example is shown by those parts of the army whom they consider as most likely to be successful in their first efforts. The Hyderabad and Jaulnah force are chiefly looked to, and the northern division of the army; and the European regiment has, from what they style its regimental grievances, become the corps from which they expect the first act of opposition. Its late proceedings

*This chiefly alludes to the officers of the corps.

are applauded and confirmed by the force at Hyderabad: and I know it was intended, if there had been the slightest indication of any coercive measures, or even had the Commander-in-Chief arrived, to have marched this corps and the two sepoy battalions in the division to effect a junction with the Hyderabad force, in order to organize an army to commence hostilities with Government. Their march was to have taken place as to-day; and it was, for five hours after my arrival, a subject of warm discussion, Whether I should be recognised or not as their commanding officer? And, after stating every thing a man could state to reclaim them to better feeling, I was obliged to give them the choice of the extreme, of either immediately submitting to the order of Government, or of opposing it. They chose at last the former; but placed it on the grounds of that general respect which was paid by them, and all their brother officers, to my character. I did not think it necessary to fight regarding the grounds of their obedience on this point, being satisfied with the substance, and particularly as I had received this proof after they were informed of my sentiments and intentions. Though an immediate open rebellion against Government has been prevented by my arrival at Masulipatam, the danger is not past; and we must not deceive ourselves, or any longer evade this serious question. The officers of the Company's army on the coast are no doubt at this moment in a state of actual insurrection against the Government; and this combination against authority is every moment maturing and spreading wider. I have seen the letter * from the Bombay army to that of the coast, and it is unqualified in its condemnation of the orders of the 1st of May, and its promise of support. Several private letters have been received from Bengal. An address from that army, to the same effect as that of Bombay, is expected: at all events they appear certain that no human power will lead the Bengal

* This was afterwards discovered to be a forgery.

oops to act against them. They calculate upon opposition from the King's army, and their plans are concerted to meet it. These deluded men are aware of the ruin they are bringing upon themselves; but their infatuation is so great, that they are reconciled to their ruin, in the expectation that it will equally involve that Government against which their rage has been so industriously and so successfully excited. All attempts to reason with men in the state of mind they are in, appears vain. Even the circulation of the able letter from Bengal is, as I apprehended, likely to inflame, instead of appeasing their passions. It is so true, that when men's minds have gone completely wrong, that which ought to put them right has, in general, a direct contrary effect: and the fact is, that all those correct principles and loyal feelings, which are so eloquently expressed in the letter from the supreme Government, but serve to impress them more forcibly with a sense of that guilt into which they have so precipitately rushed, and to render them more desperate in their proceedings, as they can (after what has passed, and particularly late events at this place,) only see individual safety in all being equally involved in the deepest guilt. I entreat you to be persuaded that these sentiments are quite general; or, at least, that the few who do not entertain them have neither the means nor the courage to oppose their progress; and allow themselves, with an indefensible passiveness, to be borne along with the tide. Under such a state of circumstances, all hopes of this spirit of insurrection subsiding must be at an end. Some steps must instantly be taken; and no good can result from the application of any partial remedy. The disease is general, and the remedy must be so also. It remains with you to decide on the measures that are to be adopted. The first and most military, though not, perhaps, the most political, that suggests itself, is the employment of actual force. In such a contest, however, not only the means must be calculated, but the result; and, as far as I can judge, success, even in this extreme, would not save us from the most baneful consequences. It seems therefore not wise to have resort to such a measure, till every other that it is possible for Government to take, without the annihilation of its own power and dignity, has been tried and failed. Unqualified concession to the demands of the army, either in dismissing public servants of Government, or in rescinding its orders, would be a virtual resignation of its power, and cannot therefore be made. It would, indeed, be better and more honourable, if *matters were at the worst*, that Government should fall by any hands than its own. Should Government not resolve on having immediate resort to force, one line only remains that could at the present moment afford a rational hope of the necessity of having recourse to that extreme being avoided, or at least of its being resorted to with advantage; which is, to meet the crisis at once, by a general order to something of the following purport:

" Government finds, with concern, that it can no longer " indulge that sanguine hope which it once entertained, " that the irritation which a variety of causes have com- " bined to produce in the minds of the Company's army " on the coast would subside; and as it is satisfied that the " evils which must result from the existence of those com- " binations against its authority, that are now formed in " almost every station, will, if suffered to continue, be as " injurious to the public interests, as if those by whom " these proceedings are carried on were in a state of open " hostility to Government; it feels compelled to antici- " pate every extreme that can occur, and to publish to " the army at large the final resolutions which it has " adopted under this extraordinary and unparalleled " situation of affairs: and these resolutions will, it is satis- " fied, be found to combine as much attention to the feel- " ings of the army as it is possible to show without a " sacrifice of the public interest, and an abandonment of " the authority and dignity of Government. The Go-

"vernor and Council can and does make every possible "allowance for feelings so strongly excited as those of the "officers of the coast army have been, and is disposed to "refer that great agitation of mind into which they have "been thrown by a concurrence of causes which must "greatly mitigate, if they do not altogether extenuate, "that degree of criminality which must always attach to "such proceedings: and, under such impressions, he can "view their extreme solicitude regarding those of their "brother officers whom he has thought it his duty to "suspend the service, with that consideration which is "due to a highly meritorious body of officers, acting under "the strong impulse of warm and honourable, but mis-"taken feelings. And with such sentiments he cannot "deem it derogatory to Government to state, that he in-"tends, in the full confidence that the officers of the coast "army will abandon their present dangerous course of "proceeding, to recommend to the Honourable the Court "of Directors the restoration to the service of those officers, "whose suspension, and the reasons which led to it, have "been reported to them, and who are consequently the "only authority by which that act can be repealed: and "he can have no doubt, but the earnest desire of their "brother officers, combined with the high character which "most of the officers under suspension formerly held, will "induce the Honourable Court to overlook their late con-"duct, and comply with this recommendation. Acting "upon the same principle, Government is pleased to "appoint Colonel Bell to the charge of the battalion of "artillery at the Mount, and Colonel Chalmers to the "command of the subsidiary force in Travancore. Lieu-"tenant Maitland is appointed quarter-master of the "European regiment of infantry.

"The committee of inquiry ordered to assemble at Ma-"sulipatam is repealed; and no act, either of any body, "or of individual officers in the Company's service, of "which no cognizance has yet been taken, and which

" occurred before the present date, will be made subject of
" future notice, or even operate to the disadvantage of
" such body of officers or individuals, unless they should,
" by a perseverance in the same course, and a repetition
" of the same conduct, forfeit all claim to such lenity and
" consideration at a moment when Government has taken
" such steps to tranquillize the agitated minds of the army,
" and to leave even the most mistaken without a plea for
" perseverance in their present dangerous course. It
" must declare its positive and final resolution neither to
" alter nor modify this proceeding. It will yield no more
" to the entreaties or demands of the army: and if any
" officers are so infatuated, and so lost to every considera-
" tion of the public good and the general prosperity of
" their country, as not immediately, on the promulgation
" of this order, to abandon their present course of proceed-
" ing, Government must, however much it may deprecate
" such an extreme, meet it with that firmness and courage
" which becomes a constituted authority of the Empire
" of Great Britain. It has contemplated this possible,
" though, it trusts, highly improbable event; and the
" different officers entrusted with command are directed,
" should any spirit of turbulence and insubordination appear
" among the officers of the troops under their command,
" to punish the individuals with all the severity of martial
" law. And should the operation of the regular course of
" justice be impeded, either by a combination among the
" officers or men, such will instantly be proclaimed rebels
" against the legal authority of Government and their
" country; as Government is perfectly satisfied that the
" public interests will receive more injury from any effort
" to conciliate men who persevere (after what has passed)
" in principles so opposite to the restoration of order and
" discipline, than it even can meet from them as open
" enemies to their King and Country."

I am aware that a thousand objections may be made to an order of this nature; but it must only be tried by the times; matters have arrived at such a crisis, that something decided must instantly be done. There is not an hour for delay. And what I have suggested is only the first proclamation in a war that seems to me, even with this step, almost unavoidable. If human means could avoid it, this act will; for it holds out every motive that can incline men to good and deter them from evil. It concedes, no doubt, in some points; but the case is urgent, and the spirit of concession is corrected by the firmness and resolution which is mixed with it. But your own mind will suggest every thing. I am, as you know, devoted to the cause of my country. It will depend upon you where I am to act, if matters draw to an extreme. I should prefer my station at Mysore, as that in which I have most influence, and could, in consequence, contribute most to the support of the public interests. I cannot conclude without again entreating you not to allow yourself to be lulled into security, and to be satisfied of the absolute necessity of taking some steps or another to save the state from the imminent danger to which it is exposed. But inaction, even dangerous as it is, may be better than the commencement of a coercive system, before steps have been taken to gain more friends to Government than it has at present in the army: and I confess I can see no mode of doing this but by a measure which is completely decided and final; and which, while it grants every indulgence even to erroneous feelings, looks to the close of this great question with a moderate and conciliatory, but a firm and manly spirit. I shall be most anxious for your sentiments, as soon as possible, on the line I am to pursue at this place. The question of the marines, and the removal of some of the officers, had, I find, (for they have shown me all their papers,) been anticipated by the other stations; and the opposition here was in part by instruction: and subsequent letters sufficiently show, that this case is no longer that one, nor of the garrison of Masulipatam, but of the whole army; and that they are most deeply pledged to the support of each other. Indeed *there cannot be a doubt* but the punishment of any one would cause the whole to break out. This I feel it my duty to avoid, as well as to prevent their marching, which was their intention, and which they expect to be called upon to do, till I know the general line you mean to pursue.

I am, my dear sir, &c.

(Signed) JOHN MALCOLM.

TO SIR GEORGE BARLOW.

(Private, and Secret.)

Masulipatam, 6th July.

DEAR SIR,

AFTER my letter of yesterday I have little to add. I can only again implore your most serious consideration to the whole question, and your instant decision on the line that is to be pursued; not merely here, but with the whole army. No half measures will at this moment answer: and unless some effort is made to appease the minds of the deluded officers of this army, you must make military preparations to reduce them to order; and these must be directed against every station under your Presidèncy: for though success may be various, an effectual opposition will be made at all; and none are more violent than some of those nearest the Presidency. If you adopt a measure of the nature that I recommended yesterday, it should be *quite final;* and therefore embrace every concession and act of conciliation *that you can make,* without a substantial sacrifice of the dignity of Government.

I can think of no improvement to this order, except

you conceive the great object of avoiding hostilities would justify the following addition to it

"Government received a representation from a number "of the officers of the coast army, in which they solicited "the equalization of their allowances with those of the "officers of the Bengal army. This is a subject, the "consideration of which must exclusively rest with the "Court of Directors, under whose notice this application "will, *in course,* be brought, and by whose decision it "will be the duty of the officers of the coast army to "abide."

This order, which is only a repetition of facts added to what I suggested yesterday, would, I think, *if firmly acted upon,* completely end the present agitation; or, at all events, you would only have a part to combat instead of the whole. Every man who was not lost to reason and loyalty would be recovered; and the few that resisted, if any did, would soon be reduced. This mode of settlement would, it may be stated, give a triumph to the army, establish a dangerous precedent, and violate fundamental principles of the Indian Government: but it is not principles, but an empire, that is in danger: and what other course can be adopted? No man can calculate the consequences of a contest between Government and its army. The delusion which prevailed, that the officers would never proceed to extremes, is now completely dissipated. I have read papers, from almost every division, calling upon this garrison to commence opposition; and I, two hours ago, read another paper from the Hyderabad force, approving of the proceedings of the garrison at this place in the cases of the marines and Colonel Innes, declaring it to be the cause of the whole, and promising full support. I knew papers of the same kind will be received, as fast as the tappals can bring them, from every station in the army, and that they are all pledged never to let a man or officer of this garrison be punished for a proceeding which they consider (and with truth) to have been caused by the general state of discontent and turbulence in the army. The garrison here are equally impelled to action by a sense of their danger from what has passed, and a desire to obtain credit with their brother officers for being the first to step forward in the common cause. My authority was at first disputed; and they have subsequently tried, by every means that men could use, to obtain from me promises of amnesty and of inaction, in the event of their being forced to move at the call of their brother officers. Such promises I have, of course, steadily refused; and I have taken advantage of every moment to diffuse better sentiments: but I should deceive you if I stated that my success went further than to keep them quiet. For the moment they are quiet; and, unless a movement is made by the Hyderabad and Jaulnah force, I think they will remain so, till some general measures are adopted by the whole: and I have (I hope not erroneously) considered, that to keep them, by any means that do not compromise my own authority or that of Government, from acting at such a moment, is an object of the greatest importance; for if any one corps begins, there is no remedy but in a war. If this was only a mutiny of the garrison of Masulipatam, it would be an easy question, and I should be proud to hazard my life in an effort to quell it to morrow morning: but one step, of any description, taken in this affair at the present moment, would undoubtedly cause a general rise in the army: and it is, I conceive, of ultimate importance, that you should know and prepare for this great political danger; and I have consequently laboured incessantly, and I hope with success, to prevent its breaking out at this most inflammable of all quarters.

The officers here have written to other stations to know whether they are to submit to the investigation of the committee. They were greatly disappointed at my not coming up, as they first expected, with powers to treat with them. They would, no doubt, have been highly flattered at such a result to their violence; and I am assured I need not state to you, that any mode would be less injurious to the interests of Government, than that of its even entering (as it once did) into a discussion with the officers of its army upon this great question. If you think you have not means to reduce the officers of this army, or if you should not like to resort to them, there is only one mode, that of issuing an order, conceding all you can, without hazard to your authority, then coming to issue in a bold and prompt manner. This, though it may be thought a concession of some points, is still an act of authority; and that character of the measure will maintain the dignity of Government, which would be altogether lost in a negotiation with its own officers.

I am aware that the opinions which I have expressed are very different from those you have heretofore maintained; but the case is altogether changed. Steps of too bold a nature have been taken, for the officers of the army to retreat; and they will immediately proceed, unless some measure is instantly adopted to arrest them in their infatuated career of guilt. The question has become entirely a practical one, and must be tried as such, as much as if the country was suddenly invaded by an enemy against whom we could use the means most calculated to repel him, without any reference to general principles or to precedent.

The fact is, that course has been tried and has failed, and another must be resorted to; and measures must be taken, when the state is in less danger, to infuse better principles, and to establish a more efficient control over our Indian armies.

TO LIEUTENANT-COLONEL BARCLAY.

(Most Private.)

Masulipatam, 7th July.

MY DEAR BARCLAY,

You will hear the substance of my late communications to Sir George; and you probably will not quarrel with the opinions I have given, though others may, who think more of maintaining consistency upon paper, than of practical Government.

I have no fear now of this garrison doing any thing, unless other parts of the army break out; and that will not, I hope, take place immediately But something must be done, as the danger of leaving them in this fermenting state increases every hour. They are, in fact, afraid to retract: and shame, despair, and hope, combine to impel them forward. I know they are hastening to their own destruction; but is it politic to let them destroy themselves, even supposing that operation did not hurt Government? Certainly not. And if that extreme can be avoided by any measure which does not substantially affect the authority of Government, it should be adopted. Let us look near this bug-bear principle of consistency, at which some men are so alarmed. The order of the 1st of May was intended to break up a desperate conspiracy against Government, which was in progress. It effected the object: and now that a conspiracy has got head of a more extensive nature, are we not to use the means which seem likely to destroy it, because they are of a different character from those used on the 1st of May, and in some respect abrogates part of that proceeding? It is assuredly the effect which should be our chief and sole object, and

I mean not in two or three weeks.

we should quarrel with no means that do not *actually* impair our strength or injure our dignity. Those I have recommended would, I think, raise both.

Tell Sir George I am incessant in my endeavours to infuse better principles. I talk with all; and can hardly myself believe the change which has in some respects been produced. I have given them no promises, I have made them no pledges; but I have told them I would take no steps but in an open manly way, and that I expected they would make no secret attempts against my authority. In this they acquiesced. I have given them all my letters regarding this unfortunate crisis, that to Doveton, &c. to read; and I have painted to them, in the strongest colours, the horrors and destruction which must follow an act of any open departure from their duty. The facts I have stated are not denied by the few among them who have sense and moderation; but even they declare to me, that they are pledged beyond the power of retracing their steps.

I wish some of those who are such resolute chamber-counsellors had gone through the two first days I did with these poor misguided men: it would have been a lesson during life.

I thank God I have established, without any compromise or concession, the authority of Government over men who had almost completely thrown it off; and I am pleased at having done this in a manner that has led those very deluded men to express gratitude for the consideration I showed to their agitated feelings. I have referred every thing to the wisdom of my superiors; and, happen what will, I can never have cause for self-reproach.

TO LIEUTENANT-COLONEL BARCLAY.

Masulipatam, 8th July.

My dear Barclay,

The only thing I have seen to day, is a letter from the committee at Jaulnah, intimating their approbation of their proceedings here, and their resolution to march the moment it became necessary to support them.

I saw a private letter from Hyderabad, stating that it was the general opinion and wish there, that Masulipatam should not be abandoned, and that two battalions and a regiment of cavalry would be sent to support the troops of this division. They consider themselves pledged to show me all papers; and they do so: but the fact is, that it is a new and important feature in this conspiracy, that they no longer think any concealment necessary. Some measures must instantly be taken with these deluded men, and Government must go as far, the first step, as it ever can go, to try and reclaim them. If little expedients or half measures are taken, all will be confusion and trouble. Depend upon it, the first King's corps that is moved, the whole commences. Their private correspondence with Bengal is now very active. I am personally here going on smoothly and well, and lose not a moment in giving better impressions: but though this may calm for the moment, and dispose them to receive any thing like a considerate decision, it will never stop proceeding.

P. S. Our little party of artillery is true; but it is the only party I yet know that can be depended upon.

TO LIEUTENANT-COLONEL BARCLAY.

(*Most private.*)

Masulipatam, 10th July.

My dear Barclay,

I shall be glad to see Sir Arthur's papers. When I wrote to Sir George, and proposed that he should, along with every decided step, make some *reappointments*, I, of course, meant to include several that I did not mention by name: but if this principle is acted upon, Government cannot be too large in their first order: any *thing little* will spoil all. Gentlemen who lose by these arrangements, should be declared, in public orders, to have the right of succession to the first vacancies.

There are more letters, advising Masulipatam to be kept: and in one of to-day from the committee at Hyderabad, I find they are equally public there in their proceedings; so I suppose you must have heard from that quarter, no order for the movement of a corps in any of these divisions will be obeyed, nor even the removal of an officer; so that the necessity of some measures being adopted is quite indispensable. Perhaps Sir George Barlow will wish to see me at Madras, with the report of the committee; but this will be, perhaps, too great a delay. Taylor or Irton should command this regiment.

I saw a letter from Hyderabad to day, written under a conviction that the Bengal army had taken up their cause. This, I have told them, is one of a thousand dangerous errors into which they are led; but I do not think they believe me, for they are completely infatuated.

TO SIR GEORGE BARLOW.

Masulipatam, 17th July, 1809.

DEAR SIR,

I HAVE this moment received a letter from Lieutenant-Colonel Barclay of the 12th instant, from which I observe, that you deem it impolitic to adopt any measures of the nature I suggested in my letters of the 5th and 6th July from this place. If I did not consider the present as one of the most serious crisis that ever this Empire was placed in, I certainly should not again intrude myself upon your notice; but I feel bold in the consciousness that I am performing a duty of the most sacred nature; and you will, I am assured, pardon the earnestness with which I solicit leave to be allowed to report to you personally the result of the proceedings here, and of all I have seen or heard connected with the general combinations in the army, as well as those means by which I think it may be averted, or its objects (if it does occur) in some degree defeated. It is quite impossible for me to convey to you in any letter the extensive information I now possess upon this subject; and I should only be four days in going to Madras, and could return, if required, with equal celerity. Little time would be lost by my making this journey; and I feel satisfied its result might be of the utmost consequence to the public interest.

Major-General Pater will be here the day after to-morrow; and no inconvenience wou'd result from the want of a high military authority: but I would not, of course, proceed, if he thought there was any urgent call for my remaining here. But such a trip would, I am assured, tend to calm, instead of irritating men's minds, as they would suppose I had gone to make a full representation of all that had passed, all that I have observed.

I entreat you to pay attention to this earnest request: and if you do that, you will order Lieutenant-Colonel Barclay to station bearers as far as Ongole. I shall lay them to that place, in the confidence that your kindness will not deny me this opportunity of endeavouring to promote the public interests by important communications.

I beg you will not conceive that I am so presumptuous as to hope to change any of those principles you have laid down for the government of your conduct: but I am convinced I can give a detailed information that will be useful, under every aspect which the present danger may assume.

I am, with respect,

Your's faithfully,

(Signed) J. MALCOLM.

TO SIR GEORGE BARLOW.

Masulipatam, 18th July, 1809.

Dear Sir,

I wrote last night, to request you would allow me to post to Madras with the proceedings of the committee, which I expect will be closed about the time I get your answer. I am most solicitous that you should comply with my request. There are circumstances connected with what has taken place here, of a nature too delicate but for personal explanation: and there are points not only relating to what is likely to be done by the deluded officers of this army, but to measures which Government may adopt to counteract their designs, that I feel satisfied I could give you the most useful information.

Should any circumstances lead you to deny my request I hope, if you contemplate extreme measures, that you will early place me in a situation where I am conscious I can, under all circumstances, be useful on the largest scale to Government. I mean at my station of Mysore. The army of that state is strong, and can be increased at a moment to any number; and I hope you will consider that at its head (should any serious misfortune occur) I am in my proper place. Here, after I have executed the objects of my mission, (which I understand to be, to prevent men rushing into open rebellion, and to make inquiry into the causes and reasons of what had passed,) I am only a regimental officer at the head of a corps, with the officers and men of which I can have no more influence than any other commanding officer would have. There is a general officer commanding on the spot, and the senior officer in the division.

I have already done all it is possible to do in disseminating good feeling among these deluded men; but they are lost to reason; and, except one or two, and those of little influence, they appear (such is their delirium) to desire the occurrence of that crisis which must end in their ruin.

I entreat you not to think that it is from any doubt of the power of Government that I am so anxious for some measure that will prevent the evils that are impending: it is from a near contemplation of all the horrors of the scene that is about to occur, and a conviction that both humanity and policy require every effort to be made, to save a brave and meritorious class of men from destruction.

If any path was opened by which men led away by a false sense of honour could retrace their steps, I believe numbers would return to Government. If nothing is done, and measures of a serious preparation or actual coercion are taken, no human power can prevent the occurrence of the most shocking scenes: and the name and reputation of this army will, whatever is the event, be lost for ever.

You will, I am sure, make allowances for my feelings: they are communicated only to you. I am distressed and unhappy to an extent I cannot describe; but I, of course, maintain a different tone to those infatuated men under my command, from whom I have not concealed my sentiments with regard to the destruction they are bringing on their own heads.

General Pater is expected to-morrow. It will now be his duty to report the state of this garrison. I shall intrude no more upon this, or any subject connected with it, until I have the honour of seeing you, which I trust will be at an early period.

I remain

Your's faithfully,

(Signed) JOHN MALCOLM.

TO LIEUTENANT-COLONEL BARCLAY

Masulipatam, 18th July, 1809.

MY DEAR BARCLAY,

I LAST night received your letter of the 12th instant, and am most happy to learn that Sir George Barlow approves of my first proceedings.

I expect that Berkeley and Evans will be here the 21st or 22d; and it is my decided opinion no investigation should be made till they arrive. This inquiry must be considered by the whole army as a regular military proceeding: and the impression made by the appointment of such a committee would be lost, if I was to execute its duties: besides, the delay is trifling. If Sir George adopts no measure which supersedes the object of this committee, I should wish to be authorized to carry the report to Madras. I will travel Dawk; and can, if required, return in the same way. General Pater will be here; and Berkeley can, if necessary, be appointed to the temporary command of the regiment; if Taylor is not brought down, *which I think he ought*, from Vizagapatam. Believe me it is of the utmost consequence I should personally communicate with Sir George Barlow upon the whole of this important subject.

I am glad Sir George Barlow has placed it at my discretion to pardon, if I thought it necessary, the non-commissioned and privates of this garrison: but no circumstance short of an open attempt to throw off my authority can ever lead me to think of such a step, as it would immediately drive to despair the European commissioned officers, on whose temper and moderation depends, at this moment, the allegiance of almost all the officers of the Company's army on the coast: for *one line* from this garrison would, to my *positive knowledge*, at this moment spread the flames of mutiny over the peninsula

Under such circumstances, of what consequence would even a triumph over a few officers at Masulipatam be, supposing that certain, unless you were prepared for contest every where? I will never abandon my authority, or fail in the performance of my duty; but I never shall (*unless positively ordered*) take any step that I conceive likely to involve my country in a civil war. Such an extreme it must be the wish of Government to avoid as long as it possibly can. Nothing, indeed, can justify its commencement, but the total failure of every possible means to prevent its occurrence.

The present combination of the officers of the Company army against the Government has hardly a feature common with an ordinary military mutiny; and therefore the principles that would apply to the one, are by no means applicable to the other. It is not the reduction of a corps

Taylor is an excellent *steady* officer, has great weight with the regiment, (particularly the men); and *though* he signed some papers, is, I feel satisfied, true to his country and the Government.

or garrison to order and obedience, but the reclaiming a large body of men to their attachment and allegiance, to the state they serve, which is the object; and this never can be done by partial measures, whether these are of a lenient or a coercive nature.

I have no doubt but Government would ultimately triumph in the contest, if it commenced this moment; but it would be a triumph over its own strength: and the occurrence of such a rupture must produce consequences that will shake our Indian Empire to its base.

From the progress of the present agitation I fear Government will not have much time for consideration*: and it should always be recollected, that in a crisis like the present every thing depends on the moment at which measures are adopted; and the same act which would be successful to-day, would perhaps totally fail of producing the desired effect if adopted a month hence.

You will satisfy Sir George Barlow, that one of the first things I did, after I came on shore, was to satisfy the minds of the officers, and, through them, of the men, of the intentions of Government in ordering a party of marines from the corps: and you will see by the enclosed extract from my journal †, that I took the first *good* opportunity that offered, of stating this fact in the most public and impressive manner to the whole regiment.

I am most anxious to hear from Sir G. Barlow, subsequent to his receipt of my letters of the 5th and 6th instant, as my mind is in a state of the most distressing anxiety. I have, however, to support me, the con-

* There are two distinct measures now in progress; one, *an appeal to Bengal;* and the other, *a plan* to obtain, by operation of a combined nature, if they cannot by remonstrance, the repeal of the orders of the 1st of May.

† I sent Colonel Barclay a copy of my speech to the regiment on the 15th of July; and yet *I am accused* by the Government of Fort St. George of not making this communication.

sciousness of having fulfilled my duty to him and to my country.

Your's ever sincerely,

(Signed) JOHN MALCOLM.

P. S. I am again ordered to Persia by Lord Minto. When will this life have an end?

TO LIEUTENANT-COLONEL BARCLAY.

Masulipatam, 18th July, 1809.

My dear Barclay,

A most violent letter was received from the committee at Hyderabad yesterday, abusing the garrison for suffering me to enter, and desiring my instant removal, unless I promised that the orders of the 1st of May should be rescinded. I have had a dreadful struggle all day; but they are at last moderated in some degree. Their present resolution is, to wait two days; but as I mean to commence the inquiry to-morrow, agreeable to the authority I have from Sir George, I trust they will agree to-morrow to remain in their allegiance till the result is known. I shall finish it in four days; and probably, if General Pater acquiesces, carry it myself to Madras. I beg you will post boys as far as Ongole. I shall return, if necessary, instantly; and I can lose nothing by the journey: and the information I shall have it in my power to give, will be of ultimate importance under every resolution Sir George takes.

Your's ever, most truly,

(Signed) JOHN MALCOLM.

TO SIR GEORGE BARLOW

Masulipatam, 19th July.

Dear Sir,

I wrote a short note to Colonel Barclay last night, informing him of the change that had taken place here, in consequence of the communication received by the officers of the garrison from the different committees of the other stations, and particularly that of the Hyderabad force, in which they were instructed to call upon me for an instant assurance that the orders of the 1st of May would be rescinded: and, if I refused to give it, to throw off their allegiance and obedience to Government; and they were assured their example would be instantly followed by every corps in the service: and part of the Hyderabad force was, they were told, ready to march to their support. The ferment which the receipt of those letters occasioned is not to be described.

I sent for some of the senior officers, and communicated my sentiments regarding the irretrievable step this garrison was on the point of taking; and pointed out, in the strongest colours, all the horrors to which it would lead. I told them I must proceed to do my duty if I found any rash resolution was taken, and that it would prove the commencement of the most horrid and unnatural contest that ever occurred. The truth of my arguments were admitted by some of those to whom I spoke; and their efforts, after a great struggle, calmed the minds of the others so far, that they agreed to wait for six days further. This, I stated, was nothing. It was, in fact, better to come to issue at once. That it had been my intention to have proceeded (in consequence of authority I had received from you) instantly into the inquiry of past transactions; and that I had meant, if I had thought there was no fear of this garrison throwing off its allegiance while I was absent, to have gone to Madras, and made this report in person; but, if their sentiments did not alter, I could not carry that resolution into execution. They stated their belief that the officers of the garrison of Masulipatam would be most reluctant to refuse assent to any proposition of mine that did not go to detach them from that general cause to which they had sworn to sacrifice their lives; and that though they knew, from what had passed, that I would give them neither promises nor pledges, nor even communicate my opinion of the probable measures of Government, they hoped there would be no objection to my proceeding; and a pledge would be given, that unless other parts of the army moved, or threw off their allegiance, that the garrison of Masulipatam would remain dutiful and obedient till I returned to communicate the resolution of Government, or till that was intimated through some other channel.

I have considered it of great importance to delay that open opposition to which this garrison has been excited by every station in the army, as I was certain, under whatever circumstances it might occur, it would be the signal for the whole to throw off their obedience. The garrison here is not more than 1,100 effective men (exclusive of the artillery); and if an effort had been successful to detach the men from their officers, who are, to a man, combined against Government, it would not have prevented the explosion; it would but have increased that despair and madness which are impelling men to these acts of disobedience: and no partial benefit that could have arisen, would have counterbalanced the general effect of this measure. Besides, I cannot speak with confidence of the success of this attempt: the *men even* of this garrison have been already debauched from their duty; and as it has been hitherto my object to reclaim the officers to their allegiance, and at all events to delay the execution of their plans, it was incompatible with the success of such a line of conduct to attempt to sound their men, or to make any private efforts to shake their attachment to their officers. Such attempts would have produced an instant open mutiny: and this, for causes before stated, I was anxious to avoid. Besides, such an expedient would have been baneful to the service, and was not to be resorted to while a hope remained of reclaiming the officers to a sense of their duty.

I hope these reasons will satisfy you of the wisdom of the part I have taken; and you must see, that unless I wish to precipitate the general revolt of the whole of the Company's army, I could not, if I remained here and waited your answer to my report, take any steps with the men to secure their fidelity: and I shall (if it is your wish I should) return to this command with your final orders, as strong, and probably stronger, in influence, (as coming direct from the seat of authority,) as I should have been, had I remained till your answer was received.

There is little chance of any thing occurring when I am away, as most stations look to this; and the result of your proceedings on the report I make will be awaited. Thus the Government will gain time, which, under every plan you can mean to pursue, must be an advantage to you, and a disadvantage to those combined against your authority. Their insanity is at this instant at its height; and every moment that action is delayed, reason has a chance of operating. Besides, their committees are likely to differ in opinions; and this is a proof of weakness some of them already begin to discover.

I have not lost a moment, as I will show you by my journal, and letter book, when I arrive, in disseminating correct sentiments, and in exposing to them in the boldest manner the true nature of that deep guilt on which they are rushing.

I have drawn their attention to a very different picture of the dangers and ruin that will attend their perseverance in this course from what they have hitherto contemplated; and though the proceedings have brought a thousand calumnies upon my head, I know great effect has been produced in the quarters where it is most essential; among the senior and thinking part, whom it has been my object to rouse; as I am satisfied, if extremes are resorted to, they will command the men.

When to all the reasons I have stated for my proceeding to Madras immediately, (that is, in three or four days from this date,) is added the advantage you may receive from the very extensive information I can give you of the temper of the army, and of their general plans of combination and action, I cannot but anticipate your approbation of this step. At all events, you must be satisfied nothing but a conscientious conviction of its being essential to the public interests could have led me to take it without your previous sanction.

I am, with respect,

Yours faithfully,

(Signed) JOHN MALCOLM.

P. S. I have, since writing the above, seen some of the senior officers, who assure me that they and their brother officers are as jealous of my honour as they would be of their own; and that if I think it necessary to go to Madras, they will pledge themselves for the orderly and dutiful conduct of the whole till my return, unless in the very unlikely case of other stations rising in arms, which they will do every thing in their power to prevent, by representing to them the pledge they have made, which they will assure them is voluntary, and has been made without the slightest promise from me. I have, indeed, cautiously avoided any communication that could lead them to believe I entertained an opinion that Government would make any concession; and the same language is held, in the private letters I have communicated to them, with regard to the actual situation of the army at this moment.

I feel now much more assured of the continued subordination of this garrison during the period of my absence than if I was present.

TO LIEUTENANT-COLONEL BARCLAY.

Masulipatam, 21st July, 1809.

MY DEAR BARCLAY,

AN account has just arrived of the opposition of the 2d of the 10th to obey the orders of Government. This has caused little sensation in the garrison, and is not expected to be followed by any movement at Hyderabad; and I feel confident now, that nothing but one of the divisions marching will make this deluded garrison stir a step further. I shall be with you on the 26th. I wish I could fly, as I am assured I can give Sir George Barlow the most complete information regarding the whole character of this wide disaffection.

Yours sincerely,

(Signed) JOHN MALCOLM.

Private Letter from Lieutenant-Colonel MALCOLM *to Lieutenant-Colonel* M^cLEOD, *dated Masulipatam, 20th July*, 1809.

DEAR M^cLEOD,

I HAVE received your kind letter of the 8th instant; but fear your hopes of my success will be disappointed. The voice of passion is alone heard; and every man that speaks with temper and reason is condemned and calumniated.

The crisis, in fact, if not arrived, appears now near at hand, when every officer in the Company's service must determine whether he will maintain his allegiance to the Government he serves, to his King and Country, or decidedly throw it off; and assuredly there is no individual who claims a title to any spirit of independence, who will not exercise his judgment upon a question which must so deeply involve all his future prospects and happiness.

If ever there was a moment in which it was important for men to look at those consequences which are likely to ensue from one step more in their course, it is the present; and it is assuredly worth while to pause for a moment, and examine coolly the nature of our grievances, and the length we are justified in going to obtain redress of them, and the probable consequences to ourselves and to our country of throwing off our allegiance to the state.

There were accounts by the last dispatches that the existence of grievances in this army was already a topic of public discussion. General M[c]Dowall and Colonel Capper have no doubt arrived before this in England, and they would be soon followed by Colonel St. Leger, and the other suspended officers. Is it not evident, that, with all the aggrieved parties in England, the public records which must be transmitted there, and the voluminous private correspondence which every ship, since those transactions took place, has carried home, that every one of the topics of complaint will be a subject of warm discussion; and will not the agitation they have created in the army be brought fully forward? and have we not reason to conclude, from all these circumstances, that an early settlement of these questions will be made by those authorities, by whom they must at all events be ultimately judged, unless this country should permanently throw off its allegiance and obedience to England? As far as we can judge from the past, there appears reason to anticipate a fair and liberal decision from the controlling authorities at home, who have certainly hitherto judged questions of this nature with great attention to both the feelings and the interests of the Indian army. With this prospect, can we be justified in resorting to such desperate extremes, because we are discontented with the acts of a temporary local Government, and not only involving ourselves in ruin, but injuring, in the deepest manner, our country, at a moment when it is the duty of every man, who has a spark of patriotism in his breast, to support her against the numerous and powerful enemies by whom she is assailed.

But we proceed, it is said, in the certainty that Government must see those evils, and that it will give way, in order to avert them; and that, indeed, it has no power, if it wished, to oppose our spirited and united demand of a full redress of grievances. Let us examine those points. Government may see great evils in our resistance of its authority, but it may perceive still greater in yielding to the peremptory demands of an armed body confederated for the purpose of intimidating it into concession. It is the extreme of the pressure, in cases of this nature, which too often causes the resistance; and as to its power of opposing any attack upon its authority, it is perhaps much greater than we at this moment calculate. There can be no doubt of the fidelity of all the King's troops to Government. It has a large body, not less than ten thousand disciplined infantry, four thousand horse, and sixteen thousand peons, belonging to the Mysore Government, all perfectly at its devotion: and it will, whenever a rupture takes place, gain, through the influence of some of the older officers, many of the native battalions. It will raise more troops. It will be compelled to promote officers from King's regiments; to give commissions to serjeants; to raise young men at once to rank, and reward with promotion all who leave their brother officers before a certain date: after which, those in arms against its authority will be proclaimed rebels; and their men, both Europeans and natives, tempted to desert and betray them by every inducement and encouragement that can be offered. All the means of Government, whatever they are, will be organized and regular; and with such it will probably triumph: but, alas! its triumph will be over its own strength. It will be in the destruction of those who are its support and glory; and, as such, must be ten times more mournful than the most signal defeat from a foreign enemy.

Let us view the other side. When men had once passed the Rubicon; and commenced opposition to Government, what would be their plans? They must be settled by distant and probably divided committees: and every young officer would feel, in such a situation of affairs, a right to examine the actions of his superiors: and could any man, under such circumstances, when the chain of discipline was broken, rely on the order and fidelity of his troops? What could be offered to induce them to resist the temptations held out by Government? And if they did not desist, would they be equal to encounter the army of the state? But say they are superior; that they were led on to victory, and all our mad passions were gratified: at what point would we arrive? Could we expect our King and Country to receive us again into favour, when our hands were red with the blood of British subjects, that we had led and assisted the natives of India to shed? And could we expect those natives would allow a few officers to continue their rule over them, after they had been taught to contemn the authority and slaughter the soldiers of the British Government? But it is stated, that we have gone so far, that to retreat would be to expose ourselves to shame and degradation. Gracious God! what an argument is this? Would men, recollecting themselves on the verge of guilt, and stopping, under the action of loyal and patriotic motives, in a career to which they had been led by strong feelings of injury, be subject of reproach or disgrace? Would it not raise their reputation higher than ever, and entitle them to look for a redress of their grievances, with a proud confidence, to that Country to which they had so strongly proved their attachment? Could it fail of exciting feelings even in the local Government, which must lead to those very conciliatory acts, which will be in vain expected, if sought with the bayonet?

This is the picture which presents itself to my mind of the scene now before us. I contemplate it with horror. And you may judge my present feelings, when I declare to God, that though I must part with those of my brother officers who are so deluded as to rush into an open warfare with the Government they serve, and their Country, I shall, I am satisfied, be happier if I fall by the first ball that is fired in this horrid and unnatural contest, than if I lived to see it terminated.

I see no possible mode in which the impending evils can be averted, but by the action of the good and loyal feelings of the majority of the officers of the army; and of this action I do not yet despair. I must, indeed, to the last continue to hope that this noble spirit will show itself, and snatch us from the gulf of destruction. I am now busy with an inquiry into past proceedings at this place, with the report of which I shall proceed in a few days to Madras; and may God grant my efforts may be useful in averting the shocking calamities that are impending!

At all events, I shall have fulfilled my duty to my brother officers, to Government, and to my Country; and that reflection will, under every event, be a consolation during my existence.

I am yours sincerely,

(Signed) JOHN MALCOLM.

N. B. An extract from a letter from Hyderabad, dated the 12th of August, 1809, from Lieutenant Watson of the artillery, to Major Morrison, at Madras, will show the effect this letter produced among the most violent at that station.

"In these troubled times it requires the full exercise of "a man's judgment upon a question which must so deeply "involve all his future prospects and happiness. Colonel "Malcolm has written at this crisis a very able and ele- "gant letter, to which a liberal consideration, I am "happy to say, has been given."

And the following passage from a letter lately received

from Lieutenant Little, at Madras, conveys a testimony, which, though probably exaggerated, is a strong corroboration of this fact.

"You may recollect, during the late unhappy disturb-"ances at this place, having wrote a long letter to "Colonel M'Leod, pointing out the melancholy conse-"quences that would finally ensue if the army continued "to persist in their opposition to Government. A copy "of this letter was sent to Captain Carfrae, at Hyderabad, "and by him shown to the force; the greatest part of "whom, a short time afterwards, declared to Major "Agnew, that they were chiefly influenced by this letter "to sign the test of obedience to Government."

No. II.

The Journal *of Lieutenant-Colonel* Malcolm, *at Masulipatam, from the 4th to the 22d of July* 1809.

4th July. Landed from the Victor sloop of war at 10 o'clock A. M. Was received by several officers, Major Storey, Captain Andrews, Captain Cotgreve, and some others, at the pier-head. As I went in at the Fort gate the European sentry stopped me, apparently to take my sword, but was ordered to desist by one of the officers. As I went to Captain Andrews' quarters I showed the orders appointing me to the command of the regiment and the garrison, as well as those for the military committee. Captain A. said he hoped I would not insist on taking the command, in the situation affairs were then in. I said I must, and desired the fort-adjutant to be sent for, to publish the orders. After we arrived at Captain A.'s house we were joined by several officers. Among others were Major Hazlewood, 24th, Captain Kelly of the 19th, and Messrs. Forbes, Nixon, and Lieutenant Spankie, of the European regiment. A long, desultory, and warm discussion took place, in which I stated all those arguments that I thought could moderate their minds and bring them to a better feeling. I particularly insisted on the consequences that must attend any of those desperate measures they had intended; and entreated them not to rush into a course which was likely to be so ruinous to themselves, and to have such dangerous consequence to their country at a moment when every man should feel it his duty to die, rather than promote, by any act, the designs of her numerous and implacable enemies. I called to their recollection, that the inquiry that was instituted was quite of a military nature, and such as they had themselves required; and that to oppose my authority, or to object to this investigation, was at once to declare war with Government. I added to this declaration an assurance, that no proceeding that was not in consistence with military usage would result from the investigation. Their answers were, for the first two hours of this discussion, made under the strong influence of passion. They had already, they said, taken their line: they knew they had gone too far to retract; and they were certain of support from the whole army, to whom they had pledged themselves. They had first expected, they said, force would be employed; and their preparations had been made in concert with the Hyderabad force to meet that emergency. They could, they said, show me the plan. I replied, with great warmth, I did not desire to see it. Such were my feelings, that I would not for the world have the guilt of such knowledge upon my mind. They recounted at great length, and with much heat, all the grievances they shared with others, and those that particularly related to the European regiment, which had been, they said, calumniated and stigmatized; one officer removed, and another banished, without a hearing: and when they remonstrated, they were told from head-quarters they *were to be disbanded:* and, after this communication, they were driven to mutiny by a large party (100 men) being ordered, professedly as a punishment, to act as marines on board his Majesty's ships. I told them, I was aware that much misrepresentation had taken place, and they might have some reason to complain; but the merits of the case could never be known without a full and temperate investigation: and it was on that account the committee was ordered, *even before the Government insisted on the marines embarking* They had therefore, as a body of officers, their choice, either to recognise my authority and allow this proceeding to take its course, or to place themselves at once in opposition to Government: there was no medium. They wished me to promise an amnesty for all that had been done here; or, at least, that I would recommend one. I said I would do neither; I would do my duty, and what I was ordered. I had thought it, I added, no departure from my duty to speak to them in the manner I had done, and should be happy if any thing I had said brought them to reason and reflection. They retired to another room; and I was informed by Major Hazlewood, that I had wrought such a change in them, that he hoped they would abandon the violent resolution they had taken.

They soon returned, and said they had done so, and submitted to my authority. Government had, they said, by the act of selecting me, taken the only step that could have stopped for an instant the course of operations which they, in concert with the whole of the Company's army, had resolved instantly to commence, in order to obtain redress of their intolerable grievances: and they desired me to understand, that it was consideration for a brother officer, who held that high place in their esteem, which he did in that of the whole army, that induced them to lay aside for the present all their schemes, and to yield him their obedience: and, as a proof of the truth of this sentiment, they declared I was the only officer of rank in India they would have admitted into the garrison; and that it had been resolved to have shut the gates on the Commander-in-Chief, had he arrived, as was once expected. I was too well satisfied with the substance of their submission to authority, to quarrel about the form of it. I in-

This was in accordance with the instructions I had received, and most assuredly marks the character of the proceeding. Yet it has been stated, I was immediately, *before investigation*, to seize the persons of the principal offenders.

stantly ordered the sentries to be taken off Lieutenant-Colonel Innes, and waited upon that officer, who I found (as was to be expected) much irritated at what had occurred: but I discovered, from his communications, too much cause for those excesses that had taken place. He is, I make no doubt, a good and a conscientious man; but his imprudence, combined with the impressions he brought from Madras, and the unguarded private communications he has since received, and made public, from a very high authority, were calculated to goad men into mutiny in common times, and could not fail of producing that effect at a moment like the present, when the whole of the Company's army is in a state of open disaffection to Government. I explained to Lieutenant-Colonel Innes the reasons that had led to my appointment, and advised him to be moderate and guarded, which he promised me he would.

I dined this evening with the mess of the regiment. There were a great number of gentlemen of other corps present. Their usual toast of "the friends of the army" was given with three times three, and I joined in it, with an observation, "that it was a very general toast, as I was "assured it included most men both in India and England." After we had sat some time, and had a number of songs, a gentlemen sung a sea-song, in which the expression "common cause" was frequently repeated. This was caught at by some of the younger officers, who were heated; and, at their motion, the whole rose to drink the "common cause." As I could not mistake the meaning they attached to this toast, I felt for a moment embarrassed, but, rising and filling a bumper, I immediately repeated, in as loud and as warm a manner as I could, "*the common cause of our Country;*" and my amendment was received and drank with acclamation. I soon afterwards left their table, and heard, as I retired, my health toasted with three times three. Thus closed the most anxious day I ever passed in my life. May my efforts be successful in reclaiming these men from the errors into which they have plunged!

5th July. I had a visit from several of the gentlemen I saw yesterday, at Mr. Savage's Gardens, (my place of residence). They seem yet to be uneasy and unsettled in their minds. They showed me several papers from different stations in the army, by most of which they were called upon to act instantly, and with a decided spirit; the strongest assurances given them of support and co-operation. Arrack for the Europeans had, I found, been sent to Gundoor, the first march towards Hyderabad; and every thing was prepared to move as to day. They again repeated their wish for some general assurance of not suffering for what had passed; and this was accompanied by some hints on the line they might be forced to pursue regarding me; though they expressed the concern with which they would have resort to such an extreme. I smiled, and said, they could not expect, from the knowledge they had of my character, that any motive on earth would ever induce me to deceive them, or to evade my duty; that to give them a promise of amnesty that I was not authorized to give them, would be deceit; and to be deterred from doing what I conscientiously thought my duty, from any fear of consequences, was, they must be satisfied, altogether unworthy of that reputation I had hitherto supported. They went away (after showing me some further papers, which they had just received, of the same character I had seen before) apparently satisfied with my answer. They communicated to me a report that had been drawn out of my conversation of yesterday, which they meant, they said, to send to Hyderabad, &c. and begged I would correct it, lest they should have misstated any of my observations. I thanked them for their candour, and corrected the paper; the circulation of which appeared to me calculated to do good.

The senior officers in this garrison are impelled to throw off their allegiance from a consciousness of having already gone too far, and seeing their only hope of individual safety in all being equally involved in the deepest guilt; while their juniors are flattered by the importance which they obtain in times of anarchy and trouble, and see nothing but distinction in being the first to step forward in what they deem the general cause of the army. I have written Sir G. Barlow my full sentiments on the present unprecedented and alarming situation of affairs.

6th July. I went into the Fort to-day, and saw the regiment under arms. I also visited the hospital and barracks. I had afterwards a long and serious conversation with an officer (A.), who spoke not his own sentiments, he said, but those of the garrison, when he entreated from me a pledge that I would not oppose any proceedings this garrison might feel itself forced to take, in co-operation with other parts of the army. I smiled at this proposition, which, as I told the gentleman, required a concession which it was altogether unworthy of me to make; and that the gentlemen who had desired him to make it would be sensible that it was so, if they gave it a second thought. I added, "I shall, however, put your minds at rest, if you will put "mine." I will take no step relative to the officers of this garrison, except in a fair, open, manly manner; and I expect, in return, they will make no secret attempts, or underhand efforts, to injure or oppose my authority. He went away, after assuring me that he was convinced what I had stated would give satisfaction, and that the officers under my command would be solicitous to show me they were deserving of that temper and consideration with which I treated them. I spoke to a number of officers to-day, and circulated a number of my private letters among them. This mark of confidence would, I knew, please; and the sentiments expressed in these papers were calculated to bring them back to reason and reflection. I wrote again fully to Sir George Barlow.

7th July. I went early into the Fort. From conversations I had with several officers, I found that I had succeeded in my efforts to restore the temper of the garrison; that they felt grateful for the moderation which I had shown; and some were sorry they had been so warm in their expressions at their first interview. I saw this day a communication from Hyderabad, and one from Jaulnah; both of which forces were prepared to support the garrison in the event of their acting in opposition to Government.

8th July. Nothing particular occurred this day. Some further communications from the westward were shown to me; one of which strongly recommended Masulipatam being kept, and not abandoned; and a force of two battalions of sepoys and one regiment of cavalry were promised to support the garrison, and the corps of the district, all of whom they appeared to think would join I entered at great length this day into the whole subject with M. H , who, *I* knew, was in intimate communication with all the senior officers, and had some influence even with the junior. I pointed out to this officer what must be the consequence of the whole or any part of the Company's army plunging down that precipice, on the brink of which they were now standing. I exposed the falseness of that confidence on which numbers were proceeding; how they would be deserted by their brethren and their men, when Government was compelled to declare them in rebellion. I pointed out how wretched their means, how unconnected their plans; and demanded, if even they had double the numbers, if he thought, after the chain of discipline was once broken, and when they were commanded by committees, and every boy thought he possessed the right to question the authority of his superior, whether it was possible to oppose the organized army that must, under all circumstances, remain with Government, and which must every day gain strength from their ranks? The whole of the king's army was, I said, decidedly with Government: and if the last step was taken, many of the Company's officers, and those probably who had the most influence with the native troops, would range on the side of authority I knew this, I said, to be fact, because I had letters, fully expressive of their sentiments, from some of the best and most popular officers in the army. I was myself, I said, of that opinion, and proud to state it. I had been in this army since I was twelve years of age; and such was my regard for my brother officers, that I would give my life to see the present unfortunate disputes happily adjusted: but if any circumstances whatever led these officers to rise in rebellion against their King and Country, and such they would do the moment they threw off their allegiance to the legal constituted authority in India, I must stand in the opposite rank: and I was convinced so many would be found of the same sentiments, that Government must triumph, though I allowed such a triumph would be one over its own strength, and consequently more mournful than the most signal defeat from a foreign enemy. I added, that I would, for the sake of argument, suppose, what I conceived impossible, that Government was destroyed in the conflict, what would be the consequence of this victory to a few officers who had led the natives of India to the murder of their countrymen and to the destruction of the British Government? Would these natives allow them to live and rule over them? or would they not be tempted to practise, for the last time, the lesson they had been taught, and get rid at once of a race whose rule they had been taught to consider as oppressive and tyrannical? Supposing they did not, would the King and people of England be ready to make peace with men whose hands were red with the blood of their countrymen? Would they not rather, if they did not abandon this quarter of India altogether, attempt its reconquest? And to what consequence would that lead? You say, I added, that your grievances are intolerable, and that if you abandon your attempts to obtain redress the coast army will be disgraced, while, if you persist with firmness and spirit, Government (which must be aware of all the consequences I have stated) must give way. To this I answer: No grievances of the description this army now has, can warrant its having recourse to arms, because they are such as must come under the cognizance of the controlling and legislative authorities in England, who are alone competent to notice and redress them: and this army, so far from being degraded by a moderate proceeding at a moment like the present, would raise its reputation higher than ever; because it would prove to all the world that it possessed a spirit of the highest loyalty and patriotism; and that when a variety of circumstances had combined to throw it into a flame, the action of these feelings had subdued every other, and it was contented rather to suffer, till the superior authorities in England could judge all those questions on which it thought itself aggrieved, than endanger the general interest of the country. Would such sentiments, I asked, redound to the disgrace or to the honour of this army? With respect, I observed, to the probability of Government giving way, if assailed with unanimity, firmness, and spirit, there was, I feared, a great and dangerous error. Government could not give way, as it was termed, beyond a certain point, without destroying itself; and it had better fall by any hands than its own. It was the very pressure, I added, that was brought against it, that forced it to resistance: and, besides, what were the points which it was required to yield? In the present agitated period of the army, every committee, every individual, had a different opinion; and if it were possible to collect the general sense of the army, I believe, in their present irritated state, concessions would be required that would amount to the virtual abolition of the existing local Government of this Presidency. It was no doubt, I observed, the duty of Government to take every step that it could take with dignity to restore temper, and to compose men's minds; but I, for one, would never blame it for refusing its consent to its own death; and such I should consider any act that made a substantial sacrifice of its strength or authority. From the answer of the gentleman to whom these observations were made, I could perceive that he and many others had been led on from step to step, without contemplating the extreme which was now so likely. It was also evident that the younger part of the army were no longer manageable: they had run away with the rest, who considered themselves too deeply pledged to retreat; and they appeared afraid of the instant obloquy that was cast on every person who withdrew himself.

9th July. As this was Sunday I went to a dressed parade of the regiment, and afterwards visited the hospital and barracks. Nothing particular occurred to-day: all the officers I saw seemed to have returned to good temper; and I can have no fear of this garrison breaking out into any extreme unless the example is given by other parts of the army.

10th July I went early into the Fort. A singular instance occurred to-day, to show how little men reflect whose minds are in a state of agitation. I was told, before I went to the Fort, that accounts had been received of every thing in Madras being in a state of confusion, and that some great event had happened there. When in the Fort, the letter that gave rise to this belief was shown me. It was dated Hyderabad the 5th July; and said a letter had that moment been received from Madras reporting the confusion which had arisen at that place; and stating that his correspondent, no doubt, "had heard of the remarkable event "that had occurred to give rise to it." The moment I saw this communication I pointed out the date; and observed it was an evident allusion to what had occurred at Masulipatam on the 25th June, which had reached Madras the 30th; and the bustle it created had been termed confusion, and sent round again, *via* Hyderabad, to Masulipatam. This was so clearly the fact, that the only astonishment that was left, was how it had not struck somebody before. By letters from Hyderabad it appears they make no secret of their proceedings. One corresponding officer writes, who says he had received a most extraordinary communication, from good authority, that the officers of the

Bengal army had sent in a Memorial to Lord Minto, praying the removal of Sir G. H. Barlow. I laughed at this unfounded assertion, and assured the person who told me, it was one of a thousand reports circulated to inflame their feelings and mislead their judgment. They have received great confidence from the address of the Bombay army*, which promises their warmest support in any measures they may take in consequence of what they deem the unjust and arbitrary order of the 1st of May.

By a letter from the committee at Hyderabad received to-day, this garrison are advised to defend Masulipatam if they can. A junction is proposed at Ongole or Condapilly. From the former station being mentioned, it would appear as if a forward movement upon Madras had been contemplated by some of the most violent.

11th July. I was with the officers of the regiment almost all this day, and dined at the mess, of which I have become a member. Our dinner was pleasant, and like that of a private party of gentlemen. I have been particularly pleased to observe, that although they communicate to me in confidence when I require it, no officer of the garrison ever begins, when I am present, any conversation on the present situation of the army; and when I speak to them upon it (as I frequently do), they are much more moderate than they were. I have seen some of the principal natives of this place, and find the events of the 25th ultimo caused a very serious alarm, which was not dissipated before my arrival. The defenceless inhabitants ascribe more influence to me than I possess, and think nothing wrong can occur as long as I remain.

12th July. Very severe rains. I did not go into the Fort, and heard nothing of consequence from any quarter.

13th July. Went into the Fort, inquired particularly from the adjutant of the regiment, and found, from his report, that the privates not only conceived they were to be

* This was afterwards discovered to be a fabrication.

dispersed and disbanded when the order came for them to go as marines, but a report was even current in the barracks, that they were going to Botany Bay. They were, he assured me, now fully satisfied of the misrepresentations that had been made to them; and he believed no discontent remained in the corps excepting that which had long existed among the men enlisted for life; and which, they had hopes, would have been altered before this, as Captain Andrews had published an order, more than a twelvemonth ago, with a view of quieting their minds; in which he stated, that Government had referred the question to England. I desired Mr. Nixon to tell the sergeants that I should inquire into this point, and do any thing in my power towards obtaining them information of what had been done upon the subject.

14th July. I this morning inspected Captain Gibson's company of artillery, and was highly pleased with their appearance. I addressed them on parade, and told them the gratification I had received from their steadiness under arms, and correct movements; adding my conviction, that they would maintain, under all circumstances, the high reputation they had acquired during the late Mahratta war. No tappal * for the last three days, owing to the rain.

15th July. A regimental court martial sat yesterday on four men, and the regiment was under arms at half past six, to see the sentences carried into execution. I judged this a favourable opportunity of addressing the corps; and, after the crimes and sentences of the prisoners had been read, I made the following short speech:

"Regiment! As this is the first time I have met you
" upon such an occasion, I forgive these men: but I
" desire you will not mistake the motives of this act of
" lenity. It is my intention, as it is my duty, to enforce the
" strictest discipline: and I must punish those that merit

* Post.

" it, not only to maintain the character of the corps, but
" to enable me to grant indulgences to the good men of it,
" which I never can do unless I punish the bad: but I
" trust, from what I have seen of your conduct, I shall
" have little occasion to exercise severity. It is, indeed,
" you must all feel, most incumbent upon you to preserve
" the utmost regularity and order at the present period. A
" late occurrence in the regiment, which has, I am satis-
" fied, been solely produced by misapprehension and
" misrepresentation, is on the point of becoming a sub-
" ject of investigation before a military court, who will
" inquire into the causes by which it was produced. I
" shall therefore say nothing on that subject: but I con-
" sider it my duty to declare to you at this moment*,
" *that it never was in the contemplation of Government to*
" *disband or disperse this corps, and that it never meant to*
" *employ any officer or man of* the regiment in any
" manner or upon any service but such as was suited to
" the honour and character of British soldiers, and which
" it, of course, conceived both officers and men would be
" forward to proceed upon. It was, soldiers, from a full
" conviction that a serious misunderstanding alone of the
" intentions of Government could have caused what has
" passed, that made me receive with pride and gratifi-
" cation my nomination to the command of this regiment:
" and I am convinced, from what I have already seen,
" that I shall (whenever I quit that station) have to make
" a report which will add, if possible, to the high reputa-
" tion which the corps already enjoys; and satisfy all, that
" as it is the first in rank of the infantry of this establish-
" ment, it is also first in fidelity, loyalty, and attachment
" to the Government it serves, and to its King and Coun-
" try."

I had watched an opportunity of making this communication in the manner I thought would have most effect. I am accused by the Government of Fort St. George of never having made it.

This address appeared to be received by both officers and men of the corps with satisfaction; and I make no doubt of its effect. I was withheld, by many and serious considerations, from haranguing the men, or publishing any explanatory order to them, on my first arrival. Such would, in the agitated state of the whole garrison, have been completely misconstrued, and would probably have produced the very opposite effect from what was intended.

16th July. I dined yesterday with the mess of the 1st battalion 19th regiment N. I., and sat till a late hour. No toasts were given; and not a word relating to the present situation of affairs escaped the lips of any man present. I could not but be pleased with such good feeling, and felt gratified at this mark of personal respect. The evening passed in the utmost hilarity and good humour.

17th July. Some of the officers of the garrison waited upon me to-day with letters of a most violent tenor that they had received from Hyderabad and other stations, in which they were reproached with weakness for having admitted me. I was described in some of these letters as a consummate politician, and consequently as the most dangerous man Government could have sent among them. The garrison were told I would *tamper with their men, cajole them*, and in the end ruin the general cause. I was happy to find the sentiments of the gentlemen who waited upon me were not in unison with those of their correspondents; but they hinted their fears of the violence of the younger officers of the garrison, who, they said, had been hurt at the speech I made to the men on the 15th, which they thought was calculated to excite the men against their officers. I appealed to an old officer of the regiment, who was present, Whether he thought the speech had any such tendency? He said it certainly had not struck him as in the least objectionable. I observed, that the testimony of an officer like him should satisfy others; and if it did not

I could not help it; for in such times a man could not put his foot over the threshhold without a misconstruction of the manner in which it was done. The officers who waited on me this day gave me a paper, the purport of which was to learn what assurances I could give them of a disposition of the Government of Madras to redress their grievances; and, in the event of my declining, to inform them what I thought the intentions of Government were. It was signified, that if I did not, the confidence of the garrison would be withdrawn from me, and they would consider themselves released from all promises they made. I told them I could make no communication of the nature they required, and that they might act as they thought proper: I should, under all circumstances, do my duty to the Government I served.

18th July. This morning M. H. waited upon me, and showed me a communication from the established committee at Hyderabad to this garrison, which called upon them to demand from me an assurance that the orders of the 1st of May would be repealed; and, if that was refused, instructed them to throw off the authority of Government, and make me leave Masulipatam. I went over all the grounds I had done before with this officer; and told him, that if the garrison was so lost to all sense of duty and propriety as to act upon this instruction, I must judge for myself, and take those steps which the emergency demanded. He said, the senior officers, who had sent him, were not disposed to attend to the call made upon them by the Hyderabad Committee; but they, he added, had now little or no control over their juniors, who were decidedly for having recourse to immediate violence. I asked him to what lengths men (who had still some reflection) meant to allow themselves to be borne away with the tide? The hour, I added, was come, when they must decide. I then pointed out the ground on which I thought they might, without injury to their honour, make a stand, and rescue the deluded young men of the army, as well as themselves, from destruction. I expressed my conviction of the men remaining with the senior officers, and that the young men must be reclaimed to reason, or at least be prevented from becoming rebels, if those who were their seniors acted with a becoming spirit. This conference lasted two hours, and M. H. went to communicate with the rest. There was, I understood, a warm discussion for several hours; after which, two of the senior officers waited upon me, and said they had with difficulty prevented the rest from coming to extremes that day; but they had at last agreed to wait six days (till the 24th), when, if they heard nothing favourable to their hopes, they meant to take such steps as they thought calculated to forward the objects they had in view. They at the same time said they had, in consequence of the opinion of their brother officers at other stations, determined to admit no investigation into their past conduct. I observed, that if these were their resolutions we must come to issue at once, and I must take those steps I judged best to counteract their measures, as I considered their proposition of adhering to their duty for a limited period of six days, was nothing less than an open defiance; and their refusal to admit investigation was a measure of the same stamp. I had meant, I said, in conformity with authority I had received from Government, to have entered into the investigation immediately (before the arrival of my colleagues); and I had entertained an intention of proceeding to Madras with the report, in the conviction that this garrison would have remained steady in its duty: but I must now, I added, abandon all such plans, and meet with that firmness which it was my duty to meet it, that dreadful emergency which this garrison had so rashly precipitated. I then read them a letter to Colonel McLeod, pointing out all the horrors of the crisis to which they were rushing. They appeared forcibly struck with what I said and read, and expressed their hope that their brother

* Vide page 149.

officers would alter their resolution, and not impede the course of proceeding which I intended to pursue. It might, they said, afford some ray of hope of the present distractions being ended; for though they knew my sentiments differed widely from theirs, and that I was devoted to my duty to Government, they were also sensible that I had warm feeling for the situation of my brother officers. I went, immediately after this interview, to dine at the mess of the regiment, and (strange inconsistency!) received every mark of respect and kindness from men who had been debating all the morning whether they should enter into a contest with me for the authority of the garrison!

19th July. I went into the Fort early this morning, and called upon Colonel Innes to give me a full statement of all that had passed relative to the origin of those discontents that terminated in the mutiny of the 25th ultimo I also called upon Major Storey, Captain Andrews, and Mr. Nixon, the adjutant of the regiment, to give me every information they had relative to these transactions. I was waited upon, soon after I went to the Fort, by two of the senior officers, who were, they said, desired by all to state that a general confidence and respect for my character had induced the garrison to change their resolutions, and that they hoped I would follow the course of inquiry I intended; and, after making the investigation, proceed, if I thought it advisable, to Madras. They would, they said, during my absence be as jealous of my honour as of their own, and promise not to depart in the slightest degree from the path of duty and order, unless a rise in other stations was to take place; of which, they said, they thought there was no probability, particularly as they would write to inform them of the pledge they had made, and entreat them not to make any call upon them before my return to my command. I told them I felt obliged by this mark of their

* I had received authority to proceed (without waiting for my colleagues) in this inquiry. Lieutenant-Colonel Berkeley had, indeed, been prevented from attending by a severe illness.

regard and confidence; but I would *not* receive it, if I thought it was made under any idea or expectation that I would be the advocate of their cause, or that of the army. They disclaimed any such idea. I would, they knew, from what they had seen, do my duty in the manner I thought best. I was gratified with the pledge I received; which, as M. H. afterwards privately observed, gave me a stronger tie on the officers while I was absent than I could have had during the same period, if present. The reasons which led me to resolve on going to Madras were fully stated to Sir George Barlow in a letter under this date.

Accounts were received this evening of the assembly of a force at Madras. I anticipated the feeling this would make, and stated to an officer present, when I received the letter, my conviction, that it was in consequence of the many, and perhaps exaggerated, reports of intended mutinies that had been consequent to that of Masulipatam.

20th July. General Pater arrived. I went to meet him, gave him a return of the garrison, and made a full and confidential report of all past proceedings. I found that the officers of standing, to whom I had spoken so much on the danger of allowing young men to take such a lead in the present discussions, had taken advantage of the good disposition of the moment, as to carry a resolution, that the garrison committee, which were mobbish meetings of the whole of the officers, should be abolished, and the proceedings to be entirely carried on by the eleven senior officers, by whose judgment all questions were in future to be decided, and who were entirely to act for themselves, and not to follow the instructions of other committees, or be influenced by the voice of any person not a member of the committee. This measure I considered as the first great step towards a return to reason and temper. I received an invitation from the garrison to dine with them on the 22d. All the gentlemen, civil and military, were invited to meet.

21st July. All was quiet. I received this day the

most unequivocal proofs of the desire of some of the senior officers to return to the right path, if furnished with any ground on which they could absolve themselves from the deep pledges they had made, and assert their right to control their juniors.

22d July. General Pater looked at the regiment on parade, and afterwards went, accompanied by his staff, to breakfast with Lieutenant-Colonel Innes.

Captain Gibson of the artillery informed me, that though he had received his leave to go to Madras, he would remain, if I advised him, at Masulipatam. I spoke with General Pater; and it was his opinion, as it was mine, that Captain Gibson should proceed. If he had been ordered to stay after his leave was made public, it would have excited suspicion, without any adequate benefit. Whether conciliatory or coercive measures were adopted, Captain Moorhouse, who succeeded to the command of the company of artillery, appeared equally, if not better, suited to the charge at that crisis. He was a brave, excellent officer, and had never for a moment even swerved from his duty; and his character was respected even by the most violent of the disaffected. Captain Gibson, on the contrary, having for a short time joined in their schemes, had, when he (very meritoriously) checked himself in his career of guilt, been considered a deserter from their cause, and had become an object of their marked hatred and resentment. General Pater dined with the officers of the garrison; and the best feeling possible was shown at this entertainment. After dinner I proceeded by post to Madras.

JOHN MALCOLM.

No. III.

TO

THE HON. SIR G. H. BARLOW, BART. & K.B.

GOVERNOR IN COUNCIL.

Fort St. George.

HONOURABLE SIR,

I HAVE this day transmitted to the Commander-in-Chief of the forces an account of the inquiry into the proceedings of the officers at Masulipatam, previous to my assuming the command at that station. I now consider it my duty to report every event that occurred during my command of that garrison. It is, however, essential to my own character and to the information of Government, that I should state the peculiar circumstances under which I proceeded on this duty, as well as the impressions which existed at that moment on my mind, respecting your intentions not only regarding the garrison of Masulipatam, but the whole army; as it is with reference to those impressions alone that my conduct in the discharge of this delicate and important duty can be judged.

I received a message to attend at your Gardens on the 1st July; and was informed, when I arrived there, of the mutiny which had occurred at Masulipatam, and of an improper and disrespectful remonstrance which you had that day received from the Company's officers of the subsidiary force in the Deckan. You did me the honour to ask my opinion on both subjects; and I suggested, that an officer of rank should be immediately ordered to Masulipatam, to inquire into, and report upon, the proceedings of the officers of that garrison; and that a letter should be written to the commanding officers of the subsidiary forces at Hyderabad and Jaulnah, informing them of your having received, with regret and disapprobation, a Memorial from the officers under their command, soliciting that you should rescind the orders of the 1st of May; and pointing out, in the most forcible manner, the dangerous tendency of such addresses, and the total impossibility of complying with their request; and directing the commanding officers to call upon the officers under their command to reflect upon the serious consequences which a perseverance in such measures must produce.

After some discussion regarding the officer it would be proper to nominate to the command of the European regiment and the garrison of Masulipatam, I offered to proceed myself upon that service; and you accepted my offer with an apparent confidence in my success, of which I could not but be proud. The emergency gave no time for the preparation of instructions, and I was immediately appointed to command the garrison of Masulipatam and the Madras European regiment; while two respectable officers, Lieutenant-Colonel W. Berkeley and Major Evans, were nominated to act with me, as members of a military committee that was directed to investigate the conduct of the garrison.

I was repeatedly assured by you, at the last interview with which I was honoured, that you committed the dignity and interests of Government (as far as those were implicated on this occasion) into my hands with perfect confidence, and that you gave me the fullest latitude of action: adding, that I was fully acquainted with your sentiments upon the whole subject of the existing discontents among the officers of the Company's army. I certainly was, from the confidence with which you had honoured me, fully aware of your sentiments. I knew that you were most solicitous to allay the ferment that had arisen in the army, and that you were at that moment resolved to use every means in your power to effect that object, but such as you deemed derogatory to the honour and dignity of the Government with which you were charged. You regarded, I knew, the occurrence of a rupture between the state and any part of its army, as one of the most desperate evils that could arise, and thought every moment that such an event was delayed was of ultimate importance, as it gave time for reflection and the action of better feeling, and strengthened the hope that deluded men might yet return to that path of duty and good order from which they had so widely departed.

The act of my appointment to Masulipatam of itself proclaimed these sentiments; and I was confirmed in them from the approbation you gave to my suggestion regarding the mode of treating the Memorial you had received from the officers of the subsidiary force, which you desired I would put into the form of a letter, and send to you; which I did, through the medium of your military secretary, Lieutenant-Colonel Barclay. Impressed with these sentiments, I sailed for Masulipatam early on the morning of the 2d of July, and arrived there on the 4th. I found the officers of that garrison in a state of open and bold mutiny against Government, with every thing prepared to march towards Hyderabad, to effect a junction with the subsidiary force at that place, by whom they had been promised complete support in the opposition they had commenced to the authority of Government. The most violent among the officers of the garrison saw, in recognising my authority, a complete suspension, if not a total discomfiture, of their plans, and argued loudly against my being acknowledged: and it was not till after a dicussion of near five hours that I was enabled to bring these deluded men to a sense of all the perils of their situation, and of the consequences that must ensue from their throwing off their allegiance to the state. They at last were subdued by the force of reason; for no other means were used, as I thought it equally my duty to avoid any promise of amnesty for the past, or of consideration for the future: and they, after repeated and fruitless trials, desisted from all applications upon these points. A repetition of the discussions which occurred at this scene (accompanied, however, with less violence) took place next day: after which, the question of disputing my authority was abandoned.

I was happy to find, by a letter from Lieutenant-Colonel Barclay, under date 12th July, that the mode as well as substance of the proceedings that I adopted on my arrival at Masulipatam was honoured with your entire approbation.

I took every opportunity of mixing with the officers of the garrison, and circulated among them a variety of letters, which I had written with a view of reclaiming the more violent of my brother officers to better feelings and better sentiments; and I found that my conversation, and the perusal of these papers, had soon a very visible effect; and that though they continued to share the general proceedings of the army, they no longer (as they had done before my arrival) thought it incumbent upon them to take the lead in an insurrection against Government, though they were excited to that measure by the most violent letters from almost every station in the army, and were also impelled to it by their own sense of danger from what had passed, which they thought would be greatly diminished when the majority of the officers of the army were sharers in the general guilt. I considered, that by effecting this change in the temper of the garrison of Masulipatam, one of the chief objects which you had in contemplation when you sent me to that garrison, was accomplished. The rupture which had recurred, and which was likely to be followed by an insurrection of a great part of the officers of the army, had been arrested in its progress, without the slightest sacrifice of the authority, or compromise of the dignity, of the state; and time was gained, which, under every view that could be taken of the subject, appeared of the greatest advantage to Government.

The first serious interruption to this progressive improvement of good feeling among the officers of the garrison of Masulipatam, was caused by a letter from an established committee at Hyderabad, which reached that garrison on the 18th July. This letter, which, like all other papers of a similar tendency, was shown to me, reproached the officers at Masulipatam with want of wisdom in having admitted me to assume the command of the garrison. The committee desired they would instantly demand from me an assurance that the order of the 1st of May would be rescinded; and, if I refused it, recommended that measures should be immediately taken to oblige me to quit Masulipatam. A paper of demands, which the Hyderabad committee termed their *Ultimatum*, and which they said they intended to forward to Government, accompanied this letter. These papers were shown to me by an officer of some rank and influence, with whom I was in the habit of confidential intercourse. He told me the senior officers of the garrison were far from approving of the sentiments of the Hyderabad committee, but much was to be feared from the violence of the juniors. I took this occasion of exposing all the fallacy of the grounds on which they were proceeding, and of impressing, in the most forcible language I could, the dangers into which many of the officers of the Company's army were precipitately rushing. As the substance of the communication I made to this officer was afterwards circulated in the form of a letter, I enclose an extract from my journal, in which it was immediately entered: and this extract will show you the nature of those arguments I used to reclaim men from their deep delusion. This communication had evidently a great effect upon the person to whom it was addressed; and he promised me he would not only communicate my sentiments to some of the most reflecting among the officers of the garrison, and obtain, through their means, the rejection of the proposals from Hyderabad, but would endeavour, in concert with them, to effect an arrangement that would exclude the younger part of the officers from any right of deliberation on the questions with which the army was now agitated; which I agreed with him would be a point of the greatest importance, and the first step towards a final settlement of existing evils.

All these measures were happily effected. An answer was sent to Hyderabad, that the officers of Masulipatam must assert their right of judging for themselves, and that they could not comply with their demand regarding me; and the garrison committees, which were mobbish meetings of the whole of the officers, were dissolved, and all future proceedings entrusted to a few of the senior officers, who were (it was agreed) not to be influenced either by the opinions of other committees, or by the opinion of any officer in the garrison not included in their number, which was limited to eleven.

I had at this period received a report that Lieutenant-Colonel Berkeley was too unwell to come to Masulipatam, and there was likely to be some delay in the arrival of Major Evans. I also found that formal examinations before a regular committee would be likely to excite an irritation, which it had been, throughout, my study to avoid. I therefore took advantage of the authority conveyed to me by Lieutenant-Colonel Barclay's letter of the 12th of July, to commence myself the investigation of the conduct of the garrison previous to my arrival.

I had always intended (provided I had obtained your permission) to have proceeded with the report of the committee to Madras, as I was sensible I should never be able to convey to you by letters the whole of that important information I had obtained of the real state and temper of the majority of the officers of the Company's army on the coast, who, though apparently united in one confederacy, were actuated by widely different motives, and took very different views of the nature of the scene in which they were engaged: and of these different shades in their situation and intentions it appeared to me most essential you should have the fullest information, as this knowledge was evidently the only basis upon which any arrangement could be made for the settlement of the whole question, without having recourse to an open and declared rupture, which I ever understood it was your earnest desire to avoid till the last extremity. As I found the changes which had been effected left me without any fear of the garrison of Masulipatam departing from their duty during my absence, I thought it my duty, after I had completed the investigation with which I was charged, to exercise that discretion which you had given me before my departure from Madras, and proceed in person to report the result of my investigation. I communicated this intention to Major-General Pater, the commander of the division, who arrived at Masulipatam on the 20th July, and it met with his fullest concurrence and approbation.

I heard, before my departure, of the 2d battalion of the 10th regiment of native infantry having refused to march; but as that event did not appear likely to be immediately followed by any open act of contumely or disobedience in the Hyderabad force, and as it produced no commotion whatever in the garrison of Masulipatam, it was an additional excitement to the resolution I had adopted, as I expected to have arrived at Madras (by travelling in the rapid manner I did) before any determination had been taken upon this act of mutiny and disobedience, and to have furnished information that might have aided your judgment in deciding upon that important question.

As I always conceived that it was the object of Government to reclaim, if possible, the minds of the officers, I directed my whole attention, during the period I was at Masulipatam, to this great object. I therefore cautiously abstained from any attempt to discover the sentiments of either the European or native soldiery. Such an attempt must have been instantly known, and would have inflicted an irremediable wound on the minds of the officers, and have been certain to precipitate that crisis which it was my labour to avoid.

To evince that I have not been deceived in the expectations I formed of the change of feeling in the affairs of the garrison of Masulipatam, I enclose an extract of a letter from an officer, in whose correctness I place entire confidence. The resolutions which the committee of Masulipatam have agreed to consider, are such, no doubt, as it would be impossible for Government to have acceded to; but they exhibit a most important change from former violence to comparative temper and moderation; and their agitation shows that these officers reject all share in the demands made in that paper which is termed their *Ultimatum* by the Hyderabad committee. It must be recollected, that in cases like the present, where the minds of a large body of men have been greatly disturbed, that their return to reason is likely to be as gradual as their departure from it: and I can have no doubt, from what I know of the present temper and inclination of some of the senior officers in the northern division, as well as in other quarters of this army, that had not the recent acts of the force at Hyderabad led to those measures which Government has thought it its duty to adopt, they would have seized with avidity any opportunity that the indulgent considerations of Government for their past errors had afforded them, of reclaiming themselves and others from the deep crimes into which they had plunged, and of restoring to its former name and glory a service which the rash madness of some of its members threaten with ruin and destruction.

It remains for me only to state, and I do it with deep regret, that, as far as I can judge, late occurrences have annihilated every hope of the garrison of Masulipatam (I speak with the exception of the artillery company) remaining faithful to its duty ; and I fear there are several corps in the division, the officers of which will be disposed to follow their example.

I entreat you to pardon the length of this letter, as well as the freedom with which I have stated my sentiments. I can have no desire but to show that I have not been false to that confidence by which I was honoured ; and that I have laboured with zeal, and not without success, (at least as far as the scene in which I was employed was concerned,) to promote the public interests.

I have the honour to be,

Honourable sir,

Your most obedient servant,

(Signed) JOHN MALCOLM.

Madras,
1st August, 1809.

No. IV.

Address of the Inhabitants of Madras to Sir George Barlow

TO

THE HON. SIR G. BARLOW, BART. & K.B.

GOVERNOR, AND PRESIDENT IN COUNCIL, OF

FORT ST. GEORGE AND ITS DEPENDENCIES.

Honourable Sir,

We, whose names are hereunto subscribed, impressed with a deep sense of our duty to our Country, and of the necessity of good order and obedience to the constituted authorities, beg leave to render you, at this moment of difficulty and danger, our assurances of support to the interests of Government, and of our readiness to devote our lives and fortunes to the maintenance of the public tranquillity in any way in which to you, in your wisdom, it may seem meet to command them.

We desire to take this opportunity of publicly expressing our fullest disapprobation of that spirit of insubordination which has recently shown itself amongst the officers of the Honourable Company's army serving under the Presidency of Fort St. George: fully convinced, that it is the duty of every good subject to yield obedience to the commands of those whom the will of his Sovereign and the laws of his country have placed in authority over him, and patiently to await the result of a reference to Europe for the redress of real or supposed grievances. Any conduct, impatient of the period of such appeal, and backward to the calls of professional obedience, we regard as subversive of all good order and discipline, hostile to the constitution of our native country, and big with danger to the existence of the British empire in India.

And we therefore, honourable sir, beg to repeat the assurances of our firm determination to resist the operation of such principles, which we are convinced must be equally reprobated and condemned by all good and loyal subjects.

Fort St. George,
9th August, 1809.

No. V.

Letter from Lieutenant-Colonel MALCOLM *to Major-General* GOWDIE, *Commander of the Forces in Chief, Madras.*

SIR,

I HAVE before informed you, that in consequence of instructions I received from the honourable the Governor, through the medium of Lieutenant-Colonel Barclay, military secretary, I proceeded (without waiting the assembly of the committee that was ordered) to make an inquiry into the conduct of the garrison of Masulipatam. I considered that the best form in which I could make this inquiry, was to collect from Lieutenant-Colonel Innes every information he could give, and to obtain such evidence from the officers of the garrison as appeared necessary to establish the leading facts of the transactions it was my object to investigate. I judged that a minute and formal personal examination of the parties was equally unnecessary to the object of the preliminary inquiry with which I was charged, and unsuited to the temper of the times, or to the fulfilment of those objects which I conceived the honourable the Governor to have had in view at the time I was appointed to the command of the garrison of Masulipatam.

The officers of the garrison whom I called upon for information, were of course cautious in committing to writing, or indeed in verbally stating, any thing that might criminate themselves: and I was induced, by many reasons, to avoid any examination of the men of the European regiment, or native battalion. Such evidence was not necessary to the establishment of the principal facts; and it could not have been obtained without a complete sacrifice of that temper which it was my object to maintain until the Government was in possession of the general result of my inquiry, and of that important information regarding the state of not only the garrison of Masulipatam, but of other stations in the army, which my employment upon this duty had enabled me to collect.

I enclose a statement given in by Lieutenant-Colonel Innes, with an Appendix, and two private notes in reply to queries I put to him, subsequent to his delivering me his first statement.

I also enclose a paper, which contains the substance of the information given me by Captain Andrews of the European regiment, and Captain Kelly of the 1st battalion 19th regiment of native infantry, and which was corroborated by several of the officers of the garrison. I transmit a paper from Lieutenant Nixon, the Adjutant, whom I examined relating to the different causes which had led to agitate the minds of the men of the European regiment, and to make them, as well as their officers, forget their duty.

You are in possession of Major Storey's public letter, stating the nature of the situation in which he was placed, and the steps which he adopted. In addition to that document I enclose the substance of a verbal declaration which Major Storey made to me upon this subject, and which shows the leading consideration which he states to have governed his conduct upon this occasion.

These enclosures will throw complete light upon the conduct of both Lieutenant-Colonel Innes and the officers of the garrison of Masulipatam: and I shall, in the course of the few observations which I feel it my duty to offer upon their contents, state such additional facts as came to my knowledge from verbal communications upon this subject.

It is not possible to contemplate the conduct of the officers of Masulipatam throughout the different stages of this transaction, without constant reference to the general discontent and disaffection to Government which, at the moment of their proceedings, prevailed in the minds of a large proportion of the officers of the Company's army on this establishment, and which must be considered as one of the chief, if not the sole cause of their excesses.

Lieutenant-Colonel Innes appears, from his statement, to have joined the corps he was appointed to command with an impression that the officers of it were disaffected to Government, and with a resolution to oppose and correct such improper principles in whatever place or shape he met them.

He landed at Masulipatam on the 7th May, and was invited on the same day to dine at the mess of the regiment; and it was after dinner, on this first day of their intercourse, that the ground-work was laid of all their future disputes. The only substantial fact adduced by Lieutenant-Colonel Innes on this occasion, and admitted by the other parties, was, that "the friends of the army" was given as a toast, at this meeting, by Lieutenant D. Forbes, and seconded by Lieutenant Maitland, quarter-master of the corps. This toast Lieutenant-Colonel Innes requested might be changed for "the Madras army;" but his proposition was not acceded to, and he, in consequence, left the table. This appears to be the only proved fact. Several observations are stated by Lieutenant-Colonel Innes to have been made by officers at the table, that were disrespectful to Government, and contrary to the principles of subordination and good order: but the only one of these observations that he specifies, is ascribed to Lieutenant

Maitland in a letter to that gentleman, which forms a number of the Appendix. In that letter, Lieutenant-Colonel Innes, after regretting that Lieutenants Maitland and Forbes had not made the apology he required of them for their conduct on the evening of the 7th May, adds, "I will still "forward any explanations you may state to me with re- "spect to the *observations you made* at the *mess* on the "7th instant so *publicly*, with respect to the *Nizam's* de- "tachment, and officers who are not friends of the army." Lieutenant Maitland, in his reply to this letter, states his hope that Government will not decide upon Lieutenant-Colonel Innes's report until he has an opportunity of defending himself: and further observes, "Until I received "your letter this day, I never knew for what words or "actions of mine an apology was required; for *I most* "*solemnly deny* ever having given any opinion, in any "manner, regarding the Nizam's detachment and its offi- "cers, that night, or at any other time, in your presence."

When Lieutenant-Colonel Innes left the mess-room, which he did, as has been before stated, in consequence of their refusing to change the toast to "the Madras army," as he had proposed, it appears the officers proceeded to drink their original toast in the manner they were accustomed to drink it, with three cheers: and these, it is not unlikely, may have been mistaken by Lieutenant-Colonel Innes for further marks of disrespect to him, and consequently to the authority by which he was appointed: but the officers of the regiment, who were present at table, deny the existence or expressions of any such sentiment.

These different statements cannot be deemed surprising, when the nature of this meeting is considered. The parties could, indeed, hardly have been personally known to each other: and although no doubt can be entertained of the goodness of Lieutenant-Colonel Innes's motives, and the laudable character of his zeal for the Government he served, it is perhaps to be regretted that his first effort to correct the principles of the officers of his corps should have been made at a convivial scene, where it was to be supposed men would be less under restraint than in any other situation, and therefore less disposed to attend to either the voice of counsel or authority.

But Colonel Innes, from his statement, appears sensible of this fact. He observes, after recapitulating the motives that led him to report *privately* the conduct of the officers of the regiment at the dinner on the 7th of May, to a confidential staff officer, from whom he received what he terms 'his original instructions,' "I at the same time particu-
"larly requested, that no *public notice* might be taken of
"what I found it expedient to state, unless I should be
"compelled subsequently to bring the business reluctantly
"forward officially; having intimated that I expected an
"apology to be tendered to me by Lieutenants D. Forbes
"and Maitland for their improper conduct on that even-
"ing, when the general orders of the 1st of May last were
"commented upon at the mess-room of the Madras Euro-
"pean regiment."

That such was the impression upon Colonel Innes's mind, is confirmed by a note from him to Mr. Nixon, the adjutant of the regiment, in which he asserts, that he made no official report of the occurrence. It appears, however, that, contrary to Lieutenant-Colonel Innes's expressed expectation, you considered it your duty to notice the private communication he had made of the occurrences of the evening of the 7th May; and the letter which the Adjutant-General wrote to Lieutenant-Colonel Innes upon that subject, under date the 17th May, was immediately put into the regimental orderly book of the corps. It would be superfluous for me to dwell upon the irritation which the measures that were adopted upon this occasion, and the mode of carrying them into execution, excited in the minds of the officers of the regiment. The nature and extent of that irritation are sufficiently explained in the accompanying documents. Its grounds were the supposed incorrectness of Lieutenant-Colonel Innes's private communications to head-quarters; the neglect with which the representations of the officers of the regiment upon this subject were treated; the hardship of a respectable staff officer being disgraced by a removal from his station, without knowing of what he was accused, or being permitted to say one word in his defence; and the unusual and extraordinary measure of detaching (as a punishment) an officer of the regiment to the command of a post where there was not one man of his corps, and the refusal of a court martial to the officer on whom this unprecedented mark of disgrace had been inflicted.

In addition to these subjects of complaint, the officers seem to have considered the publication of the letter from Lieutenant-Colonel Conway in the orderly book, as an unnecessary promulgation of the displeasure and censure they had incurred among the men of the regiment: and Lieutenant-Colonel Innes would appear to have been sensible, sometime afterwards, that this was the fact, as he desired the letter to be expunged from the orderly book.

You will observe, from the documents I enclose, all that took place connected with the appointment of Lieutenant Spankie, regarding which an impression was received by the officers of the regiment, from a communication made by Lieutenant-Colonel Innes, on the ground of a private letter, which he stated to them he had received from you, that it was in contemplation to disband the regiment, and place the officers on half-pay, if they did not alter their conduct; but that the fate of the corps would in a great degree be determined by the step which Lieutenant Spankie might take; that is, by his refusal or acceptance of the station of quarter-master. This idea (which I cannot think it was ever the intention of your letter to convey) was directly intimated by Lieutenant-Colonel Innes in the following private note to Lieutenant Spankie.

"My dear Sir,

"I believe I forgot to remark, that your "situation and Lieutenant Fenwick's are very different "now. Under existing circumstances it was equally "proper for him to decline accepting of the quarter-"mastership, as it is absolutely proper and necessary "that you should accede to the General's wishes, to save "a whole regiment. Think of this.

"Yours truly,

(Signed) "J. INNES."

This proceeding could not but greatly increase the irritation that before existed: it gave too much ground for the propagation of a belief, that the general punishment of the whole corps might depend upon the conduct of an individual (a young officer in the corps), on a question of a particular and personal nature; and it was not possible for an impression to have been made more calculated to increase the irritation and spirit of discontent which before prevailed in the regiment.

I shall now proceed to a concise view of the circumstances which relate to the order for the embarkation of a detachment of the Madras European regiment for marines, and of the occurrences which took place on the 25th June: regarding which, however, the documents already in your possession are so ample, as to require little further information upon the subject.

When Lieutenant Forbes was directed to proceed to Penang, and a party of marines, under Lieutenant Maitland, to be in readiness to embark on board the Fox frigate, no idea appears to have been entertained of opposition to these orders. Though the officers of the corps felt, that Lieutenants Forbes and Maitland being particularly ordered on these duties could only be as a punishment, and to avoid the stigma which they conceived this proceeding would bring upon the corps, they solicited Lieutenant-Colonel Innes to allow other officers to exchange with Lieutenant Maitland and Lieutenant Forbes, and at the same time assured him there was not an officer in the regiment that was not ready to take the tour of duty. This application (which proves the officers had no intention at that period of resisting the orders of Government,) was refused by Lieutenant-Colonel Innes, for reasons stated in his note to me of the 22d July, which forms a number of the Appendix.

Before the orders were received at Masulipatam for an increased number of marines embarking on board his Majesty's ships Piedmontese and Samarang, the minds of the officers of that garrison had been much inflamed by communications they had received from the different stations of the army. These expressed (agreeable to the statement of Captain Andrews and Captain Kelly) a general opinion of the illegality of the orders regarding Lieutenant Forbes and Lieutenant Maitland, and of the unjust manner in which the Madras European regiment had been treated. It was also reported from a variety of quarters, that the regiment was to be dispersed and disbanded: and these reports obtained, from the nature of preceding occurrences, a very ready belief both among the officers and men of the corps.

There can, however, be no doubt that the garrison at Masulipatam, as well as other stations with which they communicated, contemplated the detachment of so large a party as that ordered from the European regiment, as a serious diminution of their strength, and consequently injurious to the interests of the confederacy against Government, in which they were so deeply engaged; and that this consideration in some degree influenced them to that criminal course which they pursued: but I do not believe that this motive, unaided by others, would have led them at that moment to so bold and daring an opposition to orders.

The account given by Lieutenant-Colonel Innes of the proceedings of the 25th June, is, I am satisfied, perfectly correct. It is impossible for me to afford any further information than what you will derive from that document. To Major Storey's official letter, and the substance of that officer's verbal declaration to me, (which forms a number of the Appendix,) I can only add my conviction of two facts; 1st, That Lieutenant-Colonel Innes had it not in his power to coerce the obedience of the garrison in the state it was in; and, 2dly, That had bloodshed taken place, it would (as Major Storey states in his verbal declaration) have been the signal for the Company's officers at many other stations throwing off their allegiance to Government.

The accompanying deposition of Lieutenant and Adjutant Nixon is entitled to some attention. There is no doubt of the general facts which that officer has stated; they are indeed proved by the conduct of the men of the European regiment, who gave a ready support to their officers in an act which they must have known was mutinous, which it is not likely they would have done if they had not received unfavourable impressions of the intentions of Government. These impressions, however, were only the predisposing causes: the immediate impulse under which the deluded men of the regiment acted, was a wish to support officers who had been long with them, and a feeling of resentment at threatened coercion; and, under the action of this impulse, they would, no doubt, have opposed any troops that had been brought against them.

Though nothing can justify mutiny, it is impossible, when we consider that the non-commissioned officers and men of the Madras European regiment acted on this occasion at the call of almost all their regimental officers, not to acquit them in a very great degree of that share of criminality which must attach to all the individuals implicated in such proceedings. I am satisfied of the truth of what Lieutenant Nixon states regarding the discontent that exists among the men of this corps who have enlisted for an unlimited period of service. These men gave me a petition upon this subject, and prayed I would bring it to your notice. I communicated this petition to Major-General Pater, as I thought it implied, from the terms in which it was expressed, that they were aware of their situation, and were disposed to maintain their obedience to Government. It was at all events clearly to be inferred from the mode and substance of this representation, that those by whom it was made were sensible of the nature of the times, and thought them favourable for the accomplishment of their object.

It is impossible for me to state what officers have been most culpable in those irregular and unmilitary proceedings into which I have been directed to inquire; but, with the exception of those stated in Lieutenant-Colonel Innes's letter, (who had, in fact, no means of being useful,) I believe that all the officers present with the Madras European regiment, and the 1st battalion of the 19th regiment, were implicated in the general guilt. Those who took the most forward part, are stated in Lieutenant-Colonel Innes's letters.

The company of artillery stationed out of the Fort had no concern whatever in these transactions, and has remained throughout perfectly faithful to its duty and to Government.

I need hardly state that the native officers and men of the garrison of Masulipatam had no concern in this mutiny. They fell in on their parade, on the day of the 25th June, because a number of the officers of the corps called upon them to do so.

It is a justice I owe to Major Storey and to Captain Andrews, senior officer of the European regiment, to state, that from the 25th June until the 4th of July, the day on which I took the command, the utmost subordination and good order had been observed by the troops, and the duty of the garrison had been carried on with as great regularity and order as if nothing had occurred to disturb the usual routine of military discipline.

I feel it would be presumption in me to offer any opinion upon the subject of my inquiry, and I have therefore confined myself to the object of bringing before you, in as clear and concise a manner as I could, the leading and principal facts of those proceedings which I was directed to investigate.

I have the honour to be,

Sir,

Your most obedient servant,

(Signed) JOHN MALCOLM,

Lieut.-Col. Com.

Madras,
1st August, 1809.

STATEMENT *of Lieutenant-Colonel* INNES.

"TO LIEUTENANT-COLONEL MALCOLM.

"SIR,

Paragraph 1. "PREVIOUS to my being appointed to command the Madras European regiment, I was informed that the officers of that corps had given some very improper toasts on the day that Captain J. Marshall had dined at their mess here, which fully expressed their political principles, and how highly they disapproved of the previous measures of Government, adopted after Lieutenant-General McDowall's leaving Madras for Europe, whose cause and party they support.

Par. 2. "Impressed with the recollection of this circumstance, when I went to dine at the mess of the Madras European regiment, the day I landed here to assume the command, I determined neither to permit, or to pass over unnoticed, any such scene as was reported to have occurred on the day above alluded to, so extremely improper, and subversive of that high respect which is due to Government from every officer of the army of Fort St. George.

Par. 3. "What actually did take place on the evening of the 7th May last, and which rendered it not only proper, but absolutely requisite for me to quit the mess-room at an early hour, I deemed it my indispensable duty next day to communicate, in a private manner, to a confidential staff officer 'from whom I received my original instructions,' in order to show the officer commanding the army in chief, and the Honourable the Governor of Fort St. George, the violent spirit of discontent, undisguised disapprobation, and determined opposition to the measures of Government, which even then existed amongst the officers of that corps, and which was previously well known at head-quarters.

Par. 4. "I at the same time particularly requested that no *public notice* might be taken of what I found it expedient to state, unless I should be compelled subsequently to bring the business reluctantly forward officially; having intimated, that I expected an apology to be tendered to me by Lieutenants D. Forbes and Maitland for their improper conduct on that evening, when the general orders of the 1st May were commented upon at the mess-room of the Madras European regiment.

Par. 5. "The next morning I went to breakfast with Captain Andrews (who had dined at the mess the previous evening), and requested of him to acquaint the officers composing the mess, that I was under the necessity of declining to become a member of their society, 'as I had proposed,' owing to existing circumstances that did not accord with my ideas or sentiments of subordination, which was my imperious duty to restrain.

Par. 6. "Contrary, however, to my expectation, the information I had originally given was acted upon, being considered of such a tendency that it could not be passed over, as I had requested, and which ultimately led to the publication of the orders by the officer commanding the army in chief, reprimanding the officers of the Madras European regiment, removing Lieutenant Maitland from the quartermastership, and ordering Lieutenant D. Forbes to command at Condapillee; as also the appointment of Lieutenant Maitland to command a detail of the corps ordered to serve as marines, and Lieutenant D. Forbes to command a detail of the corps at Prince of Wales Island. Those measures were no doubt adopted with a view of checking any future symptoms of insubordination amongst the officers of the Madras European regiment. So far, however, from being attended with the desired effect, they only tended to increase the former state of irritation, and their determination on resistance to the orders of the officer commanding the army in chief, and Government, when their fractious arrangements were fully organized, and ready to be carried into execution by the disaffected, as has since been fully confirmed by their late and daring mutiny.

Par. 7. " When I transmitted Lieutenant D. Forbes's application to head-quarters for a general court martial, it was accompanied by my official letter, and report of the circumstances which occurred on the evening of the 24th May last, at the mess-room of the M. E. regiment, and which is now subjoined for your information ; as also the correspondence which subsequently passed between me and the officers of the Madras European regiment upon this interesting subject, now under consideration ; which I felt it my duty to forward to head-quarters for the consideration of the Commander-in-Chief, for the reasons assigned in my two notes addressed to Lieutenant and Adjutant Nixon. It only therefore remains for me to add, that what I honestly, candidly, and conscientiously stated to have taken place at the mess of the M. E. regiment on the evening of the 7th of May last, was the substance of what actually passed, and, to the best of my recollection, in nearly the same words, (or words to the same effect,) as I most solemnly declare upon my honour, and am ready to confirm upon oath.

(Signed) " J. INNES, Lieut.-Col."

" Masulipatam,
19th July, 1809."

Previous to entering upon the documents alluded to, I will call your attention to the two following paragraphs of the Governor General's letter, addressed to Sir G. H. Barlow, Bart. K. B. Governor of Fort St. George, dated

27th May, 1809; by which you will observe, I was not only *sanctioned,* but *expected* to give every information to the Commander-in-Chief and Government, (from my official situation,) which could tend to check disaffection in this division, and promote the public service either by my own example and exertions, or by applying to a higher authority to suppress it.

Par. 89. " We concur also entirely in the sentiment expressed in your general orders of the 1st ultimo, that it is not sufficient for officers holding commands to avoid a participation in such proceedings, but that it is their positive and indispensable duty to adopt the most decided measures for their suppression, and to report them to the superior authorities. The purposes of tumult and sedition may as effectually be promoted by their negative concurrence as by their active participation.

Par. 90. " The neglect of duty is an offence varying only in degree from a positive violation of it; and any officer who, apprised of the progress of disorderly proceedings among those who are placed under his immediate control, abstains from any attempt to suppress them either by the exertion of his own authority or by an appeal to the superior power, gives to those proceedings one mode of encouragement, and cannot stand absolved of blame, nor found a claim to immunity, nevertheless to a continuance of that implicit confidence which is attached to stations of authority, on the basis of so culpable and mischievous a neutrality."

(A true copy.)

(Signed) " J. INNES, Lieut.-Col."

Letter from Lieutenant-Colonel INNES *to the Adjutant-General of the Army.*

"Fort St. George.

"SIR,

Paragraph 1. "I HAVE the honour of reporting to you, for the information of the officer commanding the army in chief, and the Honourable the Governor in Council, the particulars of the daring and premeditated mutiny which occurred here on Sunday the 25th June, about two or three o'clock, P. M., when the three detachments of the M. E. regiment were ordered to embark on board the fleet as marines.

Par. 2. "On the arrival of the Piedmontese frigate, and Samarang sloop of war, at this place, I sent off a letter to Captain Foote commanding the two ships, intimating that the three detachments of the M. E. regiment were ready to embark, was he prepared and authorized to receive them on board his ships. The non-commissioned officers and privates appeared to be highly pleased at going on this duty.

Par. 3. "About sunset I observed a boat landing with some naval officers; and having invited Captain Foote on shore, went down to meet and receive him at the sea gate, to conduct him to my quarters, that we might communicate fully on every subject which could tend to promote the public service, in carrying the orders of the officer commanding the army in chief into execution.

Par. 4. "Just as the naval officers were nearly landed, I was called aside by Lieutenant Charles Forbes of the M. E. regiment, who was accompanied by Captains Kelly and Harrington of the 1st battalion 19th regiment N. I., Lieutenant and Adjutant Nixon, and Lieutenant and Quarter-Master Spankie of the M. E. regiment. Captain Kelly then read a paper, which they were deputed to communicate to me not only by the officers of the garrison, but those of this division, requesting I would postpone the embarkation of the detachments of the M. E. regiment till they could receive an answer to an address they had it in contemplation to submit to the Commander-in-Chief, and the Honourable the Governor in Council, *demanding* a redress of *grievances*. To this application I pointedly objected, having no authority to set aside the instructions I received from the Commander-in-Chief.

Par. 5. " Lieutenant Spankie then boasted of their having the most positive assurances of support from the troops at Hyderabad, Jaulnah, the Bombay army, and every division on the coast. I then observed, that I hoped those expectations would not induce them to resist the embarkation, by being guilty of mutiny, and by trying whether the troops would obey them or me. To order the whole in arrest, was *now* my *only* alternative. This, however, I could not attempt, or expect their obedience to my authority, under existing circumstances, and ' standing alone.'

Par. 6. " At this instant the purser of the Piedmontese delivered to me a letter from Captain Foote, annexed; which upon opening, it proved to be an official letter from the chief secretary of Government, dated 22d June 1809, ordering me to embark the detachment of H. M. 59th regiment of foot on board the Samarang with the least delay. I then inquired of the purser if he had not brought any other letter to me from Captain Foote? He replied in the negative, nor did he hear of any detachment being ordered on board but that of the 59th. This the deputation saw and heard.

Par. 7. " But apprehending some mistake had occurred, I told the deputation I expected a reply to my letter of that day, sent to Captain Foote, which would elucidate the subject. At 10 o clock P. M. it reached me, referring me to his letter sent by the purser. I, of course, concluded that the one from the secretary of Government was the one he alluded to, and sent Captain Foote's letter to Lieutenant and Adjutant Nixon directly: and we concluded that the detachments of the Madras European regiment were not expected to embark; which I communicated to the officers on parade next morning; adding, that they must be prepared to embark at an hour's notice in any other ships that might arrive to receive them on board, which appeared to give much satisfaction, finding they were not going by this opportunity.

Par. 8. "About 1 o'clock P. M., 25th June, the Purser, and Mr. Midshipman Shepperd, of the Samarang, returned from the Pettah to my quarters; and; to my astonishment, put Captain Foote's first and original letter (alluded to in his second) into my hand, which, by mistake, they had omitted to do the previous evening. I then expressed my regret at what had passed, although I was convinced it made no difference; as I conceived, from what passed the evening before, that the embarkation of the Madras European regiment's detachments would be resisted by the *officers of the garrison* at all events.

Par. 9. "I then sent for Lieutenant and Adjutant Nixon, showed him Captain Foote's letter, (No. 4, annexed,) and directed him to have the parties ready to go on board at 6 P. M., and to send the officers ordered on this duty to receive my instructions. I at the same time observed to the Adjutant, that, from what had passed the previous evening, I had every reason to suppose the embarkation would be resisted; and begged and conjured him to consider of the consequences; and to inform the officers, that if they would pledge their *honour* not to interfere with me in the *execution of my duty*, by carrying the orders of the Commander-in-Chief and Government into execution, it would afford me the highest satisfaction, and preserve order and tranquillity.

Par. 10. " If, however, resistance was intended to be offered by the *officers* to the embarkation, I would reluctantly be reduced to the disagreeable necessity of applying to Captain Foote of the Piedmontese to land the marines of both ships, and every seaman who could be spared, to see the orders of Government and the Commander-in-Chief *respected*, and to enable me to carry them into execution.

Par. 11. " So soon as the order for embarking was made public, and shown to the officers, they ran, in a disorderly, tumultuous, and mutinous manner, to the barracks of the Madras European regiment and the 1st battalion 19th regiment native infantry, calling on the men to arm, and prevailed on them to join them in the mutiny, and opposition to my orders, and those of the Commander-in-Chief and the Honourable the Governor in Council.

Par. 12. " Captain Kelly, Lieutenant and Quarter-Master Spankie, and some other officers, came over to my quarters, conjuring me not to insist on the embarkation, or to send to Captain Foote for assistance, which could only occasion the shedding of much innocent blood, and endangering the loss of the country. All this passed before the naval gentlemen. Their first observation was a most serious one, having got the two corps to join them in the mutiny.

Par. 13. " Another party of officers came shortly after up to my quarters, repeating what the other officers had done, and upbraiding me with giving incorrect information to Government and the Commander-in-Chief relative to what passed on the 7th ult. at the mess; on which they acted, and dispersed the regiment, on my suggestions, as a punishment, and which they never would accede to. Many other observations passed I do not exactly recollect: but I again intimated to the gentlemen, that, had they obeyed the orders issued, no mutiny could have occurred, or the public service been impeded, by their conduct and exertions.

Par. 14. " Major Storey, who had been sent for by the officers in the Fort to join in their mutiny, then came to my quarters, told me the two corps were under arms, and would not be dismissed but by a proper authority; and that he was called upon by the gentlemen to assume the command, and put me under close arrest, for the preservation of the garrison.

Par. 15. " I observed to Major Storey, that I neither could or would acknowledge his illegal arrest, and usurped authority, (although he might put me into close confinement,) for which he and the other officers would have to answer hereafter; having not only mutinied, but prevailed on the troops in garrison to do so, by ordering them under arms, (without my authority,) which they prevailed upon them to resist.

Par. 15. " Major Storey then ordered my letters to be seized that were coming from the post office, to be examined by him, and not to allow any to pass out, or any gentleman to visit me, without his permission. He then, ' I hear,' issued a garrison order, assuming the command, (as Captain Andrews did of the Madras European regiment,) and sent off letters to Hyderabad, Bombay, Travancore, and every other station and encampment that had united with them in the diabolical conspiracy against the Government of Fort St. George, as will appear on reference to the register of letters dispatched after the mutiny from the post office here; having completely laid aside the mask, publicly avowing and boasting of the support they depended upon receiving from their friends, in having their grievances redressed, imposed on them by their tyrannical Government.

Par. 17. " Here it is requisite to observe, Lieutenant Cecil, Dr. Anderson, and Mr. Assistant Surgeon Jones, of the Madras European regiment, did not join in the mutiny; nor do I think the non-commissioned and privates of the Madras European regiment, or the native commissioned, non-commissioned and privates of the 1st battalion 19th native infantry, would, had they not been *misguided* by their guilty officers, *who even* then, 'I hear,' had some difficulty to prevail on them to mutiny against my authority and that of the Commander-in-Chief and Government.

Par. 18. " Lieutenant Cecil, who commanded the main-guard, having declined on every occasion to join the other officers in their disorderly and insubordinate conduct, by resisting the measures of Government, was relieved from the duty of the main-guard by the mutineers; not, however, till he had *twice* waited on me, at the risk of his life; the second time after I was arrested, when I told him to submit, opposition being then of no use, and, being ill, to report himself sick, to avoid future ill treatment from the mutineers.

Par. 19. " Finding my letters seized by the mutineers, I sent a letter secretly to Captain Foote by his purser, with a request that copies of it might be transmitted without delay to the Commander-in-Chief and the Honourable the Governor in Council, for their information, having no other means of reporting to them till I was liberated; when a statement of circumstances would be duly forwarded, which will fully *prove* that nothing was wanting on my part to carry my instructions into execution instantly, notwithstanding the state of affairs here, so frequently reported since my assuming the command of the Madras European regiment and this division; previous to which, their opposition to the measures of Government (and confederacy alluded to,) had commenced with the Madras and Bombay army.

Par. 20. " In justice to the purser of the Piedmontese, I must here observe, that his mistake, in not delivering the letter sooner, was of no other consequence but that of delaying the mutiny a few hours, it being regularly organized, and resolved upon for some time past, and my being arrested, that I might not impede their seditious plans against Government, so actively carried on; *sorry I am to add, with too much success.* Understanding that General Pater will not reach this place before the 15th July, I forward this letter in a private and secret manner, that Government may be in possession of the fullest information on the 3d July, in case I may be put to death by the mutineers before or after the arrival of Major General Pater, commanding officer of this division.

(A true copy.)

(Signed) " J. INNES, Lieut. Col.
Commanding Masulipatam,
in charge N. D. of the Army.

Private Note from Lieutenant-Colonel INNES *to Lieutenant-Colonel* MALCOLM, *dated Masulipatam, 20th July,* 1809.

MY DEAR SIR,

I AM favoured with your note of this day's date. In reply to which I have to state, that I had no communications with the officers of the Madras European regiment on the subject of reducing the corps. But when Lieutenant Spankie waited upon me, to receive the Commander-in-Chief's letter, I intimated to him, on his refusing to accept of the quartermastership, proffered to him by General Gowdie, that if he did so, it was the General's intention to bring him to a general court martial. I at the same time conjured him to accept of the situation offered to him, as on the conduct of the officers of the regiment much depended, on this occasion; for if they persisted in the unwarrantable conduct they were now pursuing, the regiment would be reduced, and all those not on the staff put upon the half-pay of their rank. I then told Lieutenant S., that other plans, of a much more pleasant nature, were in contemplation for the regiment, which the officers seemed determined to put a stop to. I therefore begged and entreated that he and his friends would maturely and deliberately consider of existing circumstances, and study their own interest, and that of the public, by acceding to the General's wishes; which nothing upon earth could have induced me to make known to Lieutenant S. but the extreme desire I had to preserve order and tranquillity, in order to promote the benefit of the regiment and the public service. My letter from the General was a *private* one: but, I conceived, couched in such terms, as to authorize my making use of the information it contained, to check the irritation that éxisted in the corps.

Yours sincerely,

(Signed) J. INNES.

Letter from Lieutenant-Colonel INNES *to Lieutenant-Colonel* MALCOLM.

MY DEAR SIR,

WHEN I received the order of the Commander-in-Chief, appointing Lieutenant Maitland to command the first party ordered to serve as marines on board the Fox frigate, I was waited upon by Captain Yard and four subalterns of the Madras European regiment, (in the name of the corps,) requesting I would nominate any subaltern in the regiment to go in the room of Lieutenant Maitland (who was always sick at sea), or permit one to volunteer his services.

I accordingly showed the deputation my instructions and orders, from which I had not authority to *deviate;* but offered to write to the Commander-in-Chief for his permission, which they would not accede to. I at the same time assured the gentlemen, the Honourable the Governor in Council, and officer commanding the army in chief, were ready to forget and forgive every thing that had taken place; and that I would have much pleasure in accepting and forwarding any apology, 'however slight,' which Lieutenants D. Forbes and Maitland might send me; and did not entertain a doubt but should be able to get Lieutenant Maitland restored to his quartermastership, and Lieutenant D. Forbes continued with the regiment. They, notwithstanding, persisted in making *no* apology, and the subject was dropped, to my great regret.

(Signed) "J. INNES."

"Masulipatam, 22d July, 1809."

ABSTRACT *of the Evidence of Captain* ANDREWS *of the Honourable Company's European Regiment, and Captain* KELLY *of the* 1*st Battalion* 19*th Infantry, which is corroborated by several other Officers of the Garrison.*

"ON the arrival of Lieutenant-Colonel James Innes at Masulipatam on the 7th ultimo, to assume the command of the Madras European regiment, he was invited to dinner at the regimental mess, where there were several strangers present. In the course of the evening a toast was proposed, which it was conceived could not be objected to by any one, whatever might be his opinion of the recent acts of Government that have excited such general discontent amongst the officers of the coast army; viz. "The friends "of the Madras army." We were therefore much surprised to hear Lieutenant-Colonel Innes express his disapprobation of it, and his wish that it might be changed to a more general one; viz. "The Madras army." Several observed, that there were officers in this army who were not its friends, and it appeared to be the general opinion of the Company that the toast should be given out as at first proposed. Colonel Innes immediately arose from the table; and as he was going out of the mess-room, the toast was drank with loud applauses. This, we have reason to think, he construes into his being hooted out of the mess. Next day Lieutenants D. Forbes and Maitland were informed, that if they did not apologize for some observations said to be made by them at the mess in the presence of their commanding officer, their conduct would be reported to head-quarters. Those officers were, however, acquainted that they should be furnished with a copy of the report. As no specific observations were mentioned by Colonel Innes, and as those officers had neither said nor done any thing that required an apology, they of course refused to make any. When it was supposed that Colonel Innes intended to recommend himself to Government by informing them of the conversation of a convivial party, the officers of the regiment resolved to have no further communication with him, except in cases of duty. Some days afterwards, Lieutenants Spankie and Hancorn waited upon Colonel Innes, and explained to him fully their motives for declining to hold any private intercourse with him. In the course of a long conversation he repeatedly told them, that he had not reported Lieutenants Forbes and Maitland; and at last assured them, unless obliged to do so by some future conduct of theirs, he would not. With this assurance the officers of the regiment were so satisfied, that they altered their behaviour towards Colonel

Innes. His declarations, however, were equivocal and false, as will appear by the letter No. 1, which was published in the regimental orders of the 22d ult. He has acknowledged by the letter No. 2, that it was written in consequence of information communicated by him in a private letter, but which he pretended he did not think would have been acted upon. Agreeably to the orders, Lieutenant David Forbes submitted to the punishment inflicted upon him; but, previous to his departure for Condapillee, he requested the Commander-in-Chief to give him an opportunity of proving his innocence of the charge laid against him before a general court martial. The answer he received to this was, that 'the Commander-in-Chief deemed his application inadmissible:' but no reason whatever was assigned. Vide letters, No. 3 and 4. Colonel Innes put Lieutenant Fenwick's name in orders, to succeed to the situation of Lieutenant Maitland; but that officer begged leave to decline acceptance of it under the existing circumstances. The quartermastership was then offered to Lieutenant Spankie, who was told, that if he refused the situation he would be brought to a court martial; that the regiment would be disbanded, and the officers placed upon half-pay. Vide the Memorandum, No. 5, written by Lieutenant Spankie in the presence of Colonel Innes, by whom they were dictated. He was also desired to recollect the situation of Captain Yard, a married man with a large family, and to reflect upon the misfortunes he would bring down upon his brother officers; but if he would accept the appointment, there were favours for the regiment in contemplation of Government. Thus the fate of a regiment, and the favours or frowns of a Government, depended upon the will of an individual; and officers of all ranks were to be punished, if his conduct (over which they had no control) proved unsatisfactory!—Vide letter, No. 6, from Colonel Innes to Lieutenant Spankie.—On the receipt of the general order appointing him quarter-master, Lieutenant Spankie did, however, send a letter to the Honourable the

Governor in Council; and upon Colonel Innes's refusal to forward it through the regular channel, he forwarded it direct, in which he requested to relinquish the situation.—Vide letter, No. 7.—To this letter no answer was ever returned. At the same time that Colonel Innes forwarded the application of Lieutenant D. Forbes for a court martial, he transmitted an official statement of what had occurred at the regimental mess, in his presence, on the evening of the 7th ult. When Lieutenant Maitland was acquainted with this circumstance, he applied to him for a copy of such parts as concerned himself.—Vide letter, No. 8.—Colonel Innes refused to comply with this request, stating that Government would be guided by his report of that day, and decide accordingly. He also mentioned, that, as far as he knew, private information would not have been acted upon, had the expected apology been made; and he imputed to Lieutenant Maitland an observation which he said was made at the mess that evening regarding the Hyderabad subsidiary force.—Vide letter, No. 9.—Lieutenant Maitland informed him, in reply, that, until the receipt of his note of this day, he did not know for what words or actions of his an apology had been required, and most solemnly denied having made any observations regarding the Hyderabad subsidiary force on the night alluded to, or at any other time, in Colonel Innes's presence.—Vide letter, No. 10.—The letter, No. 11, was signed by every officer present with the regiment, excepting one, to whom it was not sent. On the receipt of it, Colonel Innes wrote an official note to the adjutant, in which he promised to forward the above letter, and requesting the officers of the regiment, who were present at the mess on the 7th ult., to draw up a statement of the circumstances which induced him to quit the mess-room on the evening of that day.—Vide letter, No. 12.—The letter, No. 13, is a copy of their answer. On the 2d of June arrived an order, directing Lieutenant D. Forbes to proceed forthwith to the Presidency, and there to embark for Penang for the purpose of taking charge of a few men of the regiment stationed at that island. Lieutenant Maitland was at the same time ordered to hold himself in readiness with thirty men of the regiment to go on board the Samarang sloop of war, as marines. In consequence of this order, a deputation from the officers of the Madras European regiment waited upon Colonel Innes, and earnestly requested him to select two other officers for the above duties. They strongly pressed upon him the impropriety of selecting two officers whose conduct had been branded in orders. If those gentlemen had been guilty of conduct contrary to every principle of military subordination, they were unfit to be sent on command with that stigma hanging over them; and if innocent, as the officers of the regiment asserted them to be, they ought not to be ordered from the coast until an investigation should take place, and the charge as publicly retracted as it had been preferred. It is here necessary to observe, that during the conference between Colonel Innes and the deputation, he read to them an extract from a letter received from the Commander-in-Chief, threatening the regiment's being disbanded. Respecting Lieutenants Forbes and Maitland, he said he could not select two others, as those officers had been nominated by the Commander-in-Chief. He acknowledged that he might have been mistaken as to Lieutenant Maitland's person, and that he now saw the matter in a different light to what he did at first. He also said, that the letter, No. 1, should be expunged from the orderly books; and that if Lieutenants Forbes and Maitland would offer some slight apology, he would endeavour to get the latter reinstated in his appointment. The apology was positively refused.

"Upon a candid consideration of the preceding circumstances, it will not excite surprise when we state, that alarm and indignation were excited in the minds of the officers. The false aspersions cast upon their characters might have tended to have lowered them in the opinion of the men, ignorant as they must have been of the circumstances which occasioned it. The two officers were naturally supposed to have been selected for some punishment, as Colonel Innes had publicly declared that such was the intention by their being appointed to those commands. At any rate, their feelings had been wounded by the severe reflections against them, contained in the letter of the Commander-in-Chief, which was published to the regiment. A court martial had been positively refused to the application of one of those injured officers, which was the only means he knew to clear up his character before the world.

" All the circumstances above stated took place previous to the 10th of June. We afterwards found that two more detachments were ordered from the Madras European regiment, to act as marines. We found that the officers of various stations concurred in opinion with the officers of this garrison regarding the illegality of the order respecting Lieutenants Forbes and Maitland, and the unjust treatment experienced by the Madras European regiment in general; and we heard from different quarters, that it really was intended to disband the regiment, which circumstances rendered extremely probable. On the arrival, therefore, of the Piedmontese and Samarang ships of war, a deputation from the officers of the garrison waited upon Colonel Innes, and requested him to suspend the execution of the orders regarding the three detachments of marines, until we had made a representation on the subject to the Commander-in-Chief, for the decision of the Honourable the Governor in Council. With this request he positively refused to comply, and threatened to enforce obedience to his orders by an appeal to the men. Next day he seemed determined to abide by the resolution he had expressed to the deputation, but appeared to be sensible that the officers ordered to act as marines would not be allowed to embark, and that the men respected their officers too much to go without them.

"He therefore stated, his determination to carry his orders into execution, with the assistance of the detachments of H. M. 59th regiment, the artillery, and a body of men which he said would be landed from H. M. ships then in the roads, as more particularly mentioned in the reasons signed by the deputation, and forwarded to head-quarters by Major Storey, with his official account of what occurred here on the 25th June."

APPENDIX

TO THE

STATEMENT OF LIEUT.-COLONEL INNES.

Copy of regimental Orders published by Lieutenant-Colonel INNES *in the Orderly Book of the Madras European Regiment.*

R. O. BY LIEUTENANT-COLONEL INNES.

Masulipatam, 22d May, 1809.

LIEUTENANT DAVID FORBES, of the Madras European regiment, is appointed to command at Condapilly, and directed to proceed to that station in the course of twenty-four hours after the publication of this order. The officer now in command of that garrison is directed to join his corps on being relieved by Lieutenant Forbes, who will not be permitted to be absent from Condapilly unless it becomes necessary for his health.

The following letter is published for the information of the officers of the Madras European regiment, in conformity with which Lieutenant Maitland is removed from the appointment of quarter-master, and Lieutenant Fenwick is appointed to act as quarter-master, and to take charge of the office immediately, till further orders.

To the Officer Commanding, or Senior Officer in charge of the Madras European Regiment.

Sir,

It having come to the knowledge of the officer commanding the army, that conduct highly indecorous, and contrary to every principle of military subordination, was observed at the mess of the Madras European regiment on the 7th instant, and that Lieutenant David Forbes and Lieutenant and Quarter-Master Maitland were the authors and supporters of it, I am directed to desire that you will express to the officers of the M. E. regiment the officer commanding the army's highest disapprobation of such conduct; and inform them, that a repetition of such irregularity will involve the whole corps in the severest penalty to which such insubordinate proceedings are liable; but which, however, from the benefit of your example, the officer commanding the army is yet disposed to think it will be unnecessary to resort to. Notwithstanding this hope, the officer commanding the army feels himself called upon to mark, by a suitable example, the authors of the exceptionable conduct that has come to his notice; and, with that view, has taken upon himself to anticipate the sanction of the Honourable the Governor in Council for the removal of Lieutenant Maitland from the situation of quarter-master of the Madras European regiment. For this purpose, I am directed by the officer commanding the army to desire. that you will remove Lieutenant Maitland from the charge of the appointment of quarter-master of the regiment, and that you will yourself appoint to succeed him the subaltern officer whose conduct you most approve, and forward his name to this office, that the officer commanding the army may recommend to Government to confirm your selection. Lieutenant David Forbes you will be pleased to appoint to command at Condapilly, and direct him to proceed in twenty-four hours after the publication of your orders, directing the officer now there to return to join his corps. And it is the officer commanding the army's further orders, that Lieutenant Forbes may not be permitted to be absent from Condapilly, unless it become necessary for his health.

(Signed) J. H. S. CONWAY,
Adjutant-General.

Adjutant-General's Office,
17th May, 1809.

No. II.

Copy of a Letter addressed to Lieutenant Nixon, *Adjutant of the Madras European Regiment.*

Dear Sir,

I previously intimated to you, and some of the other officers of the corps, that I would not report what passed on the 7th instant at the mess *officially*. That I mentioned the circumstances *privately*, I acknowledge, knowing that if I omitted to do so, other accounts would soon reach Madras. I have now stated the circumstances officially to head-quarters.

Yours truly,

(Signed) J. INNES, M. E. Regt.

Masulipatam,
24th May, 1809.

No. III.

Copy of an Application from Lieutenant D. Forbes *for a Court Martial.*

TO LIEUTENANT-COLONEL INNES,
COMMANDING THE MADRAS EUROPEAN REGIMENT.

Sir,

As the information which the officer commanding the army in chief has received of my conduct at the regimental mess on the evening of the 7th instant must have been extremely incorrect; in vindication of my character, I have requested, in the accompanying letter, a public investigation, and beg you will forward it to the Adjutant-General of the army.

(Signed) D. FORBES,
Lieutenant of the Madras European Regiment.

Masulipatam,
22d May, 1809.

TO THE ADJUTANT-GENERAL OF THE ARMY.

Sir,

Having been accused, in the copy of a letter from you, published in regimental orders of the 22d instant, of being one of the "authors and supporters "of conduct highly indecorous, and contrary to every "principle of military subordination," I beg leave to request, that I may be allowed the privilege of being allowed attempting to prove my innocence of that most serious charge before a general court martial; and I have to request that you will lay this my desire before the officer commanding the army in chief.

(Signed) D. FORBES,
Lieutenant of the Madras European Regiment.

Masulipatam,
22d May, 1809.

Letter from Lieutenant-Colonel Innes *to the Adjutant-General of the Army.*

Fort St. George.

Sir,

I have the honour herewith to transmit to you an official note, received last night, from Lieutenants D. Forbes of the Madras European regiment, with one to your address; both of which I request may be submitted to the Commander-in-Chief.

If Lieutenant Forbes's application is complied with, every young officer under my command will soon be making similar applications to head-quarters.

The gross and public disrespect shown by Lieutenants D. Forbes and Maitland, of the Madras European regiment, at the regimental mess of that corps, on the night of the 7th instant, so derogatory to the dignity of the Honourable the Governor in Council and Commander-in-Chief, from the observations made by these officers on the Government orders and those of the Commander-in-Chief, then received, dated 1st May; as also on the steady conduct of the native troops at Hyderabad, which was instantly noticed by me, calling upon Lieutenant D. Forbes to change the *toast* he proposed from the *friends of the army* to that of the *Madras army*, which was pointedly rejected, and the former one repeated, with three times three, obliging me to quit the mess-room; and for which improper conduct Lieutenants Forbes and Maitland subsequently declined to make an apology. I therefore feel it now my duty to report the circumstance officially, for the information of the Honourable the Governor in Council, and Commander-in-Chief.

(Signed) JAMES INNES,

Masulipatam,
24th May, 1809.

Lieut.-Colonel commanding at
Masulipatam.

Letter from the Adjutant-General to the Officer commanding the Northern Division of the Army.

Sir,

The officer commanding the army requests you will nominate Lieutenant Maitland, of the Madras European regiment, to the command of the detachment of that corps ordered to serve as marines on board his Majesty's ship the Fox; and that you will direct Lieutenant D. Forbes, of the Madras European regiment, to proceed forthwith to the Presidency, for the purpose of embarking for Prince of Wales Island, to take charge of the corps doing duty there.

(Signed) J. H. CONWAY,
Adjutant-General.

Adjutant-General's Office,
27th May, 1809.

IV.

Copy of the Reply to the Application of Lieutenant D. Forbes.

TO LIEUTENANT D. FORBES,
MADRAS EUROPEAN REGIMENT.

Sir,

I have the honour to annex, for your information, extract of a letter received from the officer commanding the army in chief.

(Signed) J. INNES,
Lieut.-Colonel in Charge of the Northern Division of the Army.

Masulipatam,
5th June, 1809.

EXTRACT, *dated Adjutant-General's Office, 31st May,* 1809.

"IN reply to Lieutenant Colonel Innes's letter of the 24th instant, I have the honour to inform you, that Lieutenant D. Forbes's letter, applying to be tried by a general court martial, has been submitted to the officer commanding the army, who deems that officer's request inadmissible."

(A true extract.)

(Signed) J. INNES,
Lieut.-Colonel in Charge of the Northern Division of the Army.

No. V.

Memorandum written in the Presence of Colonel INNES, *and dictated by him.*

"1st. Provided I (Lieutenant Spankie) do not accept of the situation of quarter-master to the Madras European regiment, I must be brought to a court martial for disobedience of orders.

"2dly. If I (Lieutenant S.) still persist in refusing the situation, the regiment will be reduced, and every officer not on the general staff placed on half-pay.

"3dly. In the event of my accepting this situation, other plans of a much more pleasant nature have been in contemplation for the regiment, which the officers seem determined to put a stop to."

No. VI.

Copy of a Letter from Lieutenant-Colonel INNES *to Lieutenant* SPANKIE.

MY DEAR SIR,

I BELIEVE I forgot to remark, that your situation and Lieutenant Fennick's are very different now. Under existing circumstances it was equally proper for him to decline accepting of the quartermastership, as it is absolutely proper and necessary that you should accede to the General's wishes, to serve a whole regiment. Think of this.

Yours truly,

(Signed) J. INNES.

No. VII.

Copy of a Letter from Lieutenant SPANKIE *to the Honourable Sir* G. BARLOW, *Bart. K. B. Governor in Council, Fort St. George.*

HONOURABLE SIR,

I HAVE the honour to request you to accept my resignation of the situation of quarter-master of the Madras European regiment. I have signed an official paper, in which I have declared, that I conceive Lieutenant Maitland has been removed from his appointment in consequence of an erroneous report of his conduct having come to the knowledge of the Commander-in-Chief, and this is still my decided opinion. On this account, and to prevent my being removed on private information, without having an opportunity of getting my conduct publicly investigated, I hope you will do me the favour to comply with my most earnest request to be permitted to relinquish a situation which I cannot hold, and at the same time retain the good opinion of my brother officers.

(Signed) J. S. SPANKIE,
Lieutenant of the Madras
European Regiment.

No. VIII.

Copy of a Letter from Lieutenant MAITLAND *to Lieutenant-Colonel* INNES.

SIR,

I HAVE this moment understood that you have found it necessary to report my conduct to the Commander-in-Chief. As I am not conscious of any misconduct, it is probable I may have something to allege in my defence; I therefore beg leave to request a copy of your report, or at least to be made acquainted with its purport.

(Signed) G. G. MAITLAND,
Lieutenant of the Madras European
Regiment.

Masulipatam,
24th May, 1809.

No. IX.

Copy of a Letter from Lieutenant-Colonel INNES *to Lieutenant* MAITLAND.

SIR,

UNDER existing circumstances, I deem your application inadmissible. Government will be guided by my report of this day, and will decide accordingly. So far as relates to yourself, you may apply to the Adjutant-General of the army for a copy. I am left to regret that you and Lieutenant Forbes did not make the *required apology* for your conduct on the 7th instant. Had you done so, as I requested, private information would not have been acted upon, as far as I know. Matters must now take their course. I will still forward any explanations you may state to me with respect to the *observations you made* at the *mess* on the 7th instant, so *publicly*, with respect to the Nizam's detachment, and officers who are not friends of the army.

(Signed) J. INNES, Lieut.-Col.

No. X.

Copy of a Letter from Lieutenant MAITLAND *to Lieutenant-Colonel* INNES.

SIR,

I AM sorry that circumstances exist to subject me to be condemned unheard for a time. I hope Government will not decide upon your report until I have an opportunity of defending myself; which, according to your letter, I must look for from the Adjutant-General of the army. Until I received your letter this day, I never knew for what words or actions of mine an apology was required; or I most solemnly deny ever having given any opinion, in any way, regarding the Nizam's detachment and its officers, that night, or at any other time, in your presence.

(Signed) G. G. MAITLAND,
Lieutenant of the Madras European Regiment.

Masulipatam,
24th May, 1809.

No. XI.

Copy of a Letter from the Officers of the Madras European Regiment to the Adjutant-General of the Army.

Sir,

It was with the most extreme concern that in our regimental orders of the 22d instant we found a copy of a letter from you, by which we were informed, that it had come to the knowledge of the officer commanding the army, that conduct highly indecorous, and contrary to every principle of military subordination, had been observed at the mess of the Madras European regiment on the 7th instant. We beg leave to assure you, for the information of Major-General Gowdie, that it appears to us that the account he has received of the conduct of those officers, who were present at the mess on that evening, must have been erroneous.

We cannot help lamenting that such a stigma on the character of so numerous a body of officers as we form, should have been thus publicly thrown out, before we had been furnished with a copy of the report that has been made against us.

We have seen, with the deepest regret, two of our brother officers punished, without being specifically informed what part of their conduct at the regimental mess induced the officer commanding the army to suppose them to have been guilty of the serious crime with which they are charged ; and we naturally feel considerable apprehension lest " the whole corps should," in a similar manner, " be " involved in the severest penalty to which insubordinate " proceedings are liable." We trust, therefore, that you will state to Major-General Gowdie our confident hope that he will have the goodness to direct us to be furnished with a copy of the information which he has received regarding the conduct observed at the mess on the night of the 7th instant. When we receive this, we have no doubt of being able to convince the officer commanding the army in chief, that the conduct of those who were present on that occasion did by no means merit the severe censure with which it has been marked.

Signed by all the Officers present with the regiment, except one, to whom it was not presented.

Masulipatam,
27th May, 1809.

Letter from Lieutenant-Colonel INNES *to the Adjutant-General of the army.*

SIR,

I HAVE the honour to forward to you an address from the officers of my corps, which they wish to be submitted to the Commander-in-Chief.

To elucidate the subject, I now transmit a copy of my note written to the officers of my corps the moment I got their letter yesterday ; and when I receive the document called for, it shall be handed to you directly, with every comment I deem requisite to make on it. They go herewith.

(Signed) JAMES INNES,
Lieut.-Col. M. E. regiment, in charge N. D. of the army.

Masulipatam,
28th May, 1809.

Copy of a Letter from the Adjutant-General to the Officer commanding the Northern Division of the Army.

SIR,

I HAVE had the honour to submit your letter of the 28th ult. with its enclosures, to the officer commanding the army, by whom I am directed to acquaint you, that he regrets you should have entered into any correspondence with the officers of the M. E. regiment on the subject, or deemed it necessary to forward their letter to head-quarters, as his decision was not adopted without due consideration, and is final.

If Lieutenant Forbes's presence is required by the Court of Inquiry now sitting at Masulipatam, you will be pleased to order him to attend.

(Signed) J. H. CONWAY,
Adjutant-General.

Adjutant-General's Office,
8th June, 1809.

(True Copies.)

No. XII.

Copy of a Letter from Lieutenant-Colonel INNES *to Lieutenant and Adjutant* NIXON.

SIR,

I HAVE the honour to acknowledge the receipt of an address from the officers of the Madras European regiment to the Adjutant-General of the army, which shall be forwarded to be submitted to the officer commanding the army in chief. I have therefore to direct, that a *statement* of the *circumstances* which passed on the 7th instant in the mess-room of the Madras European regiment, may be made out by the gentlemen of the corps now present, who dined at the mess-room on that day, which obliged me to quit the mess-room of the corps. No apology was ever subsequently made to me, although required and expected, by Lieutenants D. Forbes and Maitland, (as it was their duty to do,) for the pointed disrespect shown by them to the dignity of the Honourable the Governor in Council, and Commander-in-Chief, in my presence, their immediate commanding officer.

(Signed) J. INNES,

Lieut.-Col. M. E. regiment, in charge N. D. of the army.

Masulipatam,
27th May, 1809.

No. XIII.

Copy of the Reply of the Officers of the Madras European Regiment to the above Letter.

TO LIEUTENANT-COLONEL INNES,

COMMANDING THE MADRAS EUROPEAN REGIMENT.

Sir,

Agreeably to your orders, communicated to us by Lieutenant and Adjutant Nixon, we have the honour to state, that we were present at the regimental mess on the evening of the 7th instant, and that it was with considerable astonishment we observed you leave the mess so abruptly. We are unable to say what was the occasion of your doing so. "The friends of the army" was proposed as a toast, and we conceived it to be one that would not have been objected to; but as you wished to alter it, and rose from table when it was about to be drank, we conjectured it had given you offence, and that it was on this account you left the mess. So far from observing any pointed disrespect, we did not notice any disrespect whatever, shown by Lieutenant D. Forbes or Lieutenant Maitland to the dignity of the Governor in Council, and Commander-in-Chief, in your presence; and until we see the account you have forwarded on the subject to head-quarters, we shall be at a loss to suppose what part of their conduct on the night alluded to appeared to you to be exceptionable.

Signed by all the Officers present
with the mess on the 7th instant.

SUBSTANCE *of the Deposition of Lieutenant* NIXON, *Adjutant.*

LIEUTENANT and Adjutant Nixon informs Lieutenant-Colonel Malcolm, that the best opinion he can form, from his communication with confidential men, is, that the non-commissioned, rank and file, of the Madras European regiment, were alarmed in consequence of the measures adopted towards their officers, Lieutenants D. Forbes and Maitland, and the threat held out in the Adjutant-General's letter, (published in the regimental orderly book,) lest the most severe penalty might be inflicted on the regiment; conjecturing that they must either be disbanded, transported, or other ways disposed of, by way of punishment, on a repetition of similar conduct of their officers. To use their own expression, it was a general saying, "that they "might as well order out one of us to be flogged or "hanged up:" and certainly, in my opinion, from that period great discontent prevailed amongst the men. This discontent considerably increased from the order respecting the marines nominating Lieutenant Maitland in particular, and directing Lieutenant D. Forbes to proceed to Penang; and afterwards by two other detachments being ordered on marine service, to which they said, that they did not enlist to come to India as marines. They were also led to believe, from the ship's boat that landed here, that no marines were required for the ships in the roads, but that they wanted seamen only, and consequently supposed they were to be turned over to the navy. These points were most deeply impressed upon their minds by a communication which was believed to have come from the high authority of the Commander-in-Chief, that the regiment was to be disbanded, and the officers put on half pay, in case Lieutenant Spankie should not accept of the station of quarter-master.

Lieutenant Nixon further states, that considerable discontent exists in consequence of the great number of men in the regiment who enlisted for general service, " time " unlimited," prior to Mr. Windham's act; and that they consider it a hardship that they should not be admitted to the full benefit of the act in point of limited service.

Another cause of discontent is, that the regiment has not its tour of duty in the field, and change of station, with his Majesty's corps.

Masulipatam,
21st July, 1809.

No. XIV.

EXTRACT *from a Letter dated 28th May,* 1809.

TO LIEUTENANT NIXON,

ADJUTANT MADRAS EUROPEAN REGIMENT.

SIR,

I HAVE the honour to acknowledge the receipt of your note of this day's date, with the statement I thought proper to order to be made out in my note of last night to you, for the information of the officer commanding the army in chief. I shall now merely confine myself to remarking to the officers whose names appear to the letter now received, that had they not made observations on the late general orders of the Honourable the Governor in Council and Commander-in-Chief, and remarks on the steady conduct of the officers of the subsidiary force at Hyderabad, as also on officers "in the army" who are not the *friends of the army*, I should not have quitted the table at mess-room *merely* because "the friends of the army" was proposed as a *toast*, which I requested might be changed to the *Madras army;* and when not acceded to, I felt myself called upon to quit the mess-room. Very fortunately there were many strangers present at dinner, as well as myself, whose recollection of what passed on that day may be able to elucidate this subject, should the Honourable the Governor in Council and Commander-in-Chief deem it requisite to call upon them for this purpose.

(Signed) JAMES INNES,
Lieut.-Col. M. E. Regiment, in charge N. D. of the Army.

EXTRACT *from Division Orders, by Lieutenant-Colonel* INNES, *dated* 1st *June*, 1809.

"A DETAIL, consisting of a subaltern, 2 sergeants, 2 corporals, and 30 privates, belonging to the Madras European regiment, to be held in readiness to embark at a short notice on board the Fox frigate, to serve as marines. The officer commanding the Madras European regiment will give the requisite orders for the equipment of the above detail, which Lieutenant Maitland is appointed to command.

"Lieutenant D. Forbes of the Madras European regiment is relieved from the command of Condapillee, and directed to proceed forthwith to the Presidency, for the purpose of embarking for Prince of Wales's Island, to take charge of the detail of the corps doing duty there.

" Ensign Dickson, 1st battalion 19th regiment native infantry, is reappointed to command at Condapillee, and directed to proceed to that station with the least delay, to relieve Lieutenant D. Forbes of the Madras European regiment. The detail above named is to be struck off garrison duty.

(Signed) " JAMES INNES,
" Lieutenant-Colonel, in charge
" of the N. D. of the Army."

EXTRACT *from Regimental Orders.*

" Madras European Regiment, 2d June, 1809.

" A roll of the detail ordered on board the Fox frigate, to serve as marines, to be sent to the paymaster, to enable him to furnish them with a pay certificate. The roll alluded to, when ready, is to be inserted in the regimental orderly book. Every thing requisite from the regimental stores to equip the detail, is to be indented for directly, that the whole may be prepared to embark at an hour's notice. Pay is ordered to be issued to the detail alluded to above.

" The commanding officer has approved of the arrangement made for the detail directed to embark; but as Lieutenant Maitland has expressed a wish to the adjutant to make some exchanges of the non-commissioned officers, accedes to the wishes of Lieutenant Maitland, provided the officers commanding the companies to whom they belong consent to the exchange; otherwise those already ordered will go."

EXTRACT *from General Orders, 2d June.*

" PAY in advance for June, and arrears for May, to be issued to the troops under orders of embarkation in the course of this day, to enable them to prepare for their passage to the Presidency in the Fox frigate."

EXTRACT *from Regimental Orders, Madras European Regiment, dated 3d June,* 1809.

" THE adjutant will furnish Lieutenant Maitland with a roll of his detachment; and officers commanding companies are directed to send to that officer the pay advanced (as in yesterday's orders) for the detachment ordered as marines."

EXTRACT *from Division Orders, by Lieutenant-Colonel* INNES.

" LIEUTENANT DIXON of the 1st battalion 19th regiment native infantry, having joined his corps this morning with the detachment from Condapillee, is directed to resume the command of that station to morrow, to relieve Lieutenant D. Forbes, in conformity with the Division Orders of the 1st instant, and will be provided with a passport by the acting fort-adjutant.

(Signed) " JAMES INNES,
" Lieutenant-Colonel, in charge
" of the N. D. of the Army."

" Masulipatam,
" 5th June, 1809."

EXTRACT *from Regimental Orders, Madras European Regiment, June 6th,* 1809.

"THE commanding officer having taken upon himself to grant family certificates to the detail ordered on board his Majesty's ship Fox, Lieutenant Maitland is requested to refer to the last order issued upon this subject, which it will be requisite to attend minutely, to prevent retrenchments hereafter."

EXTRACT *from Division Orders, by Lieutenant-Colonel* INNES, *7th June,* 1809.

"THE detail ordered from the Madras European regiment is now reduced to 1 subaltern, 1 sergeant, 1 corporal, 1 drum, and 26 privates,—in all 30,—to be held in readiness to embark at a moment's notice on board the Samarang sloop of war, hourly expected.

(Signed) "J. INNES,
"Lieutenant-Colonel, in charge
"of the N. D. of the Army."

EXTRACT *from Garrison Orders, 13th June,* 1809.

"LIEUTENANT D. FORBES of the Madras European regiment being summoned as an evidence, by an Ensign Baker, to attend the Court of Inquiry ordered to assemble for the purpose of investigating the conduct of Ensign Baker, Lieutenant D. Forbes is consequently directed to remain here till further orders."

EXTRACT *from Garrison Orders, 20th June,* 1809.

"THE detail from the Madras European regiment, ordered to be held in readiness to serve as marines on board the Samarang sloop of war, are directed to join their respective companies, and to do garrison duty till further orders; but to be considered as under Division Orders to embark on a short notice."

EXTRACT *from Division Orders by Lieutenant-Colonel* JAMES INNES, *dated 23d June,* 1809.

"Two detachments from the Madras European regiment to be held in readiness to embark, at a short notice, on board of such of his Majesty's ships as may be prepared to receive them, to serve as marines, and to consist of the following strength; viz.

"One detachment, to be composed of 1 lieutenant, 2 sergeants, 3 corporals, and 35 privates; making a total of 41.

"The other, of 1 lieutenant, 1 sergeant, 2 corporals, and 27 privates—31 total. Such men as wish to have family certificates are to be provided with them by the officers under whose command they may be placed immediately.

"No time being fixed for the embarkation of the above details, they are to be considered on the strength of the garrison, (as also Lieutenant Maitland's party,) till further orders.

(Signed) "JAMES INNES,
"Lieutenant-Colonel, in charge
"of the N. D. of the Army."

EXTRACT *from Regimental Orders, June 24th,* 1809.

"LIEUTENANTS LAWLESS and CARBERY to indent for ammunition and every thing requisite to complete their respective detachments directly.

"Should Lieutenant-Colonel Innes receive any additional information from the ships, he will write to Lieutenant Nixon instantly."

SUBSTANCE *of a Verbal Declaration made by Major* STOREY.

MAJOR STOREY declared to Lieutenant-Colonel Malcolm, that he was fully satisfied, that if Lieutenant-Colonel Innes had persisted in the plan he adopted for the coercion of the garrison, there must have been immediate bloodshed; and he (Major Storey) was assured, from what he knew of the general temper of the officers of the Company's army at the moment, that such an occurrence, whatever was its issue, would have produced an insurrection against the authority of Government in many other quarters. This belief, Major Storey declares, was the chief motive that made him take the step he did.

FINIS.

J. MOYES, PRINTER,
Greville Street, Hatton Garden, London.